EAST ANGLIAN FOOD & WINE is the second book by Brigitte Tilleray, author of FRENCH FOOD À L'ANGLAISE, published last year (October 1986) by Corgi at £3.95.

It is the first of a new series on British regional cookery.

Brigitte Tilleray, a daily newspaper columnist and magazine writer, comes from Normandy but, after 20 years on this side of the Channel, is convinced that the British have some of the best natural products and ingredients in the world.

Her next book, SOUTH COUNTRY FOOD & WINE, will also be published by Partner Publications.

EAST ANGLIAN FOOD & WINE

To the people of East Anglia

A PARTNER PUBLICATIONS BOOK

ISBN - 1 - 870640 - 00 - 4

PRINTING HISTORY
Partner Publications edition published 1987

This book is set in 11/12 Plantin

Partner Publications
24 Chiswick High Road, Chiswick, London W4 1TE
Tel. (01) 994 8582
Marketed by John Oliver Book Sales
79 London Road, East Grinstead, Sussex RH19 1EQ
Tel: 0342 311842
Distributed by Carryfast Ltd

Made and printed in Great Britain by Richard Clay Ltd
part of the St. Ives Group, Bungay, Suffolk NR35 1ED

EAST ANGLIAN FOOD & WINE

Brigitte Tilleray

My sincere thanks to all the food and wine producers and retailers of East Anglia, the various national food and tourist industry organisations, the private companies and the many individuals who so willingly helped me with the research for EAST ANGLIAN FOOD & WINE

PARTNER PUBLICATIONS

'I wholeheartedly welcome *East Anglian Food & Wine.* Brigitte Tilleray's voyage of discovery should inspire all of us to explore the extraordinary variety of foods and wines as well as intriguing recipes — all virtually on our own doorsteps.

It is entirely in the spirit of our objectives at Food From Britain that iniatives like this book should prosper and I wish this book and its sequels every success.'

Walter Goldsmith, Chairman, Food From Britain.

'The Women's Farming Union extends the warmest of welcomes to *East Anglian Food and Wine.* East Anglians are proudly aware of their region's natural blessings and its cornucopia of good foods but it is with chagrin we must admit that it takes a Frenchwoman to tell us how to make the most of them! There it is though, each to his own; our French partners have a glorious history of culinary skill to harness with East Anglia's superb produce. Surely that is the ideal "l'Entente Cordiale"!'

Joy Richardson, Chairman - East Anglian Branch W.F.U.

'With a father who was born and raised in Fakenham, Southwold as my favourite peaceful unspoiled regular holiday resort and my love of fish and all involved in catching, marketing and retailing it, East Anglia means a lot to me. I congratulate Brigitte Tilleray for so expertly singing its praises and for featuring the fruits of the sea . . . the most natural of foods.'

Denys Bradfield,
Secretary of the National Federation of Fishmongers.

'Brigitte Tilleray has captured the tradition of East Anglian cuisine as seen through the eyes of a Frenchwoman. She has obviously a great love of the region. Good luck to her.'

John Adlard, Chairman, British Goose Producers Association.

'As traditional farmfresh turkey producers who conscientiously work for six months to produce one meal - Christmas lunch - we are delighted that Brigitte Tilleray has chosen to write a series of cookery books on British foods and recipes. *East Anglian Food & Wine* superbly re-creates the eating and drinking habits of yesteryear yet manages to capture the mood and eagerness of today's discerning consumer who is increasingly demanding natural, healthy, tasty, home-produced fayre prepared by traditional methods.'

David Browning,
Chairman, Traditional Farmfresh Turkey Association

‘I am delighted that you were able to say on the cover ‘that we can find virtually everything we need in Britain today . . . .’ And I am delighted to see you have included so many pork and pork product recipes.’

Amber Beever,
Chairman, Lincolnshire Branch, Women’s Farming Union

‘On behalf of the British Quality Vegetable & Salad Association I am delighted to recommend this excellent book. There is a wealth of super quality vegetables and salads grown in East Anglia, and because farmers and growers are skilled in speedy distribution of their crops almost all are available in any high street in the U.K.. So please do have a go at some of the recipes in this book. And remember that there are a wealth of exciting new or unusual crops to help make an ordinary meal a bit more special.’

Andrew Charlton, Secretary, British Quality Vegetable & Salad Association, Louth, Lincolnshire.

‘Meat is one of the most naturally produced foods available, and an important part of any balanced diet. Brigitte Tilleray’s book highlights the versatility of British pork, beef and lamb in East Anglian cuisine.’

Terry Smith,
Head of Eastern region, Meat & Livestock Commission

‘We worked quite closely with Brigitte Tilleray in the local publicity and promotion of her earlier book *French Food à L’Anglaise.*

Our previous extensive marketing experience in international book publishing, plus our newly-found expertise in East Anglian bookselling, leads us to believe that Brigitte Tilleray is not only a culinary expert with a good writing talent but she could also be destined for international acclaim.

With our added involvement in the promotion of tourism in this region, we feel confident that Brigitte’s new book will have great appeal to the visitors to East Anglia as well as to the resident population.

James and Jane Cornwall, The Ceres Bookshop, Swaffham.

CONTENTS

Introduction

Leave London from any of the eastern exits and within miles you will enter the gentle peace of the East Anglian countryside. No dramatic hills from which to admire panoramic views but instead field after field of rich and varied colour, charming soft valleys, salt marshes, languid estuaries, clusters of jealously kept villages and, above all, the immensity of the endless sky with clouds flowing towards the sea.

To tend this unique landscape, the people of East Anglia . . . hard-working farmers, fishermen, local traders, all treasuring their land as much as their past. It is from their ancestors that they have learnt to exploit the richness of their soil and make this unique, immense corner of Britain into one of the most prolific food bowls of the nation.

If modern machinery has helped some to turn their great fields into the granary of Britain, for others the tools of their trade are as ancient as their profession.

There are the fishermen who ignore the elements and provide great amounts of the fish and shellfish consumed daily all over Britain. There are the market gardeners who grow vegetables, fruit and soft fruit to perfection; poultry, pig and cattle farmers who choose to ignore the short cuts of fast breeding but instead concentrate on the quality of their product. And there are the estate owners who have introduced and so well looked after the numerous species of game thriving on their land.

They are all helped by the climate. For this flat land which is not so flat, this cold corner of the country which is not so cold, is in fact blessed by a unique almost continental climate – cold the winters can be, but all year round relatively dry and sunny. The same climate is to be found on the eastern side of France and the western side of Germany, and it is why, under the loving supervision of its owners, the vineyards of East Anglia are so prolific. Forty or more, scattered all over the East Anglian counties provide a pleasant and fruity white or rose wine.

What else can I say except that I am proud to be now part of this rich land, happy to turn my trips to farms, mills and harbours into culinary adventures.

From the old East Anglian recipes I have come across it is obvious that great use was made of the local products. Eating habits and diets have changed over the years, but let's explore with all these fine ingredients and self confidently turn all the delicious native products into a new form of East Anglian Food and Wine.

The wines of East Anglia

I am not much of a drinker but I do like good wine and, just as important, its availability for use in the preparation of certain dishes. How wonderful it is that some devoted and determined people have decided that if the Romans and Normans could grow grapes and make wine in England, then so can the English in the 20th century. It has all happened during the 20 happy years I have spent in this sceptred isle. And not surprisingly, East Anglians—a sturdy and enterprising people—have been to the forefront, blessed with Britain's driest and sunniest climate and suitable soils.

Today there are almost 50 vineyards in East Anglia, the majority producing wine for commercial consumption to one degree or another. On a total of more than 300 acres, East Anglia currently produces well in excess of half a million bottles of highly drinkable wine a year and the acreage and the output keeps on growing. In a good year, some of the East Anglian wine growers will produce up to 4,000 bottles per acre. It has not been easy. As one of the biggest East Anglian wine growers told me: 'If you are in Bordeaux or in the Moselle and you want to start a vineyard of your own, you can look at what the neighbours are doing. You can profit from the experience of hundreds of years and be fairly sure of getting it right first time.

'When we decided to go into commercial production in England over 10 years ago, all we had to go on were general guidelines about the basic potential suitability of certain vines and what analysis appeared to show was compatible soil. Then there is the amazing changeability of the English climate . . . and there were plenty of other problems to do with bureaucracy that I wouldn't want to bore you with.'

I think there is a wealth of splendid English understatement in all that. The fact of the matter is that today I can go and buy good dry or medium white wine, rose or 'light red' for the table or the pot and they are 100 percent English. Our little cottage in Norfolk is near two of the most northerly East Anglian vineyards and nothing gives me greater pleasure than to invite friends to share a bottle of the 'vin du pays'.

Now that the English have started again to produce home-grown wine on a commercial basis, I can see little to stop them. Standards are high, the wines stand comparison with their continental counterparts and a significant measure of their success is that many are now available through retail outlets in most parts of the country. After the early, and often costly years of experimentation, there are now some well-established varieties of grape that have proven their worth in East Anglian soil: the Muller Thurgau, Madeleine Angevine, Bacchus, Huxelrebe, Schonburger, Auxerrois, Rivaner, Seyvel, Pinot Noir, Reisling Sylvaner and the Austrian variety Zweigeltrebe.

This book, about East Anglian produce and recipes of all kinds, came out of a meeting at a London food and wine exhibition with Simon Alper, of the Chilford Hundred Vineyard, the biggest of the producers in Cambridgeshire. Simon, who spent several years in Beaune to learn the ancient skills of wine-making, has a splendid tale to tell of the first time the vineyard at Linton, near Cambridge, produced a serious vintage after the long 'nursery' period. Visiting friends in the Contentin province of Normandy, he and his father Sam produced a bottle to a somewhat dubious French family. The wine was poured, glasses were raised, sips taken and the father of the French family said incredulously: 'Mais c'est du vrai vin.' The Alpers, père et fils, were delighted of course.

In the village of Purleigh near Chelmsford in Essex the Greenwood family now have 38 acres under vine from a modest start in 1969. Under the New Hall Vineyards label they produce three whites, a dry red and also a 'Methode Champenoise' sparkling wine. Son Piers spent three years with the fabled house of Hugel in Alsace, producers of fine wine since the 17th century. At Bruisyard, near Saxmundham in Suffolk, the Berwicks produce up to 50,000 bottles of white wine a year from the Muller Thurgau planted in 1974/5 and Mrs Eleanor Berwick is secretary of the East Anglian Wine Growers Association. At Elmham Park in Norfolk Robin Don was also in the forefront of the revival of wine growing in East Anglia with a first commercial vintage in 1974 and from three sites over seven acres produces a very dry white and a medium dry white wine.

I have mentioned only four of the dozens of wine producers in East Anglia but I have tried most of the products of the others, too, and find them all acceptable for one reason or the other. Some, more fruity, remind me of the Alsace, others of certain dry white Burgundy, yet others of the Moselle. The range is now considerable and the wines of East Anglia are excellent with the shellfish, fish and meat products produced so bountifully in the region.

Shellfish

Shellfish

From the North Norfolk coast to Leigh-on-Sea in Essex, shellfish abounds. As a health conscious mother, it always gives me pleasure, when I go to my local Norfolk market on Saturday, to watch children spending their pocket money on a small tub of cockles of shrimps rather than lots of sweets.

The shellfish stalls are such an appetising sight: mounds of pink and brown shrimps, cockles, mussels, crab, lobster, oysters, whelks all surrounded, in the summer, by the delicious 'asparagus of the sea' the samphire.

Eat any shellfish at its plainest state with bread and butter or turn it into elaborate recipes, it does not matter; it is all there, very fresh, very regional a delicious accompaniment to all the dry local white wines.

CRAB

From April until the late Autumn, 30 to 40 boats will be leaving the beach at Cromer to fish the fabled Cromer crab. 'We fish crab from Sheringham to Trimingham' said one of the fishermen. While he was loading the shanks of pots filled with bait onto his boat, I learnt that May, June and July is really the big landing season. No wonder so much dressed crab is available all through Norfolk during the summer months. The meat of the North Sea crab is tasty and tender and can be the basis of many succulent dishes.

Buttered Cromer Crab

(an ancient English recipe)

Ingredients for 4

1 Cromer crab per person
Fresh breadcrumbs
4oz (120g) butter
A handful chopped parsley and chives
Pepper and Cayenne pepper to taste
Lemon juice

Pick the crab meat out of the shells and claws, mix together with the fresh chopped herbs and one good tablespoon of fresh breadcrumbs. Mix with pieces of butter, season with pepper and Cayenne pepper as well as the lemon juice. Pack the mixture into the shells and cover the top of each one with a little more breadcrumbs. Place a small piece of butter over each crab and bake in a moderate oven until golden brown (400°F, 200°C, gas mark 6).

Devilled Crab with Mushrooms and Celery

Ingredients for 4

1 medium crab per person
2oz/60g butter
2 spring onions finely chopped
2oz/60g button mushrooms, chopped
One large stick of celery, chopped
½ tsp Colman's horseradish dry Mustard
½ tsp white pepper
1 tablespoon Worcestershire sauce
1 tablespoon flour
2 tablespoons double cream
2 tablespoons dry white wine.

Pick the crab meat out of the shells and claws. Saute the spring onions, mushrooms and celery in 1 oz of butter. Add pepper, dry mustard and the Worcestershire sauce. Now melt the remaining butter in a saucepan. Mix the flour stirring well, then add the cream and white wine, stir well. Away from the heat add the crab meat. Mix all ingredients together. Divide the mixture into each crab shell and bake for 5 minutes in a warm oven (425°F, 220°C, gas mark 7). A small amount of grated cheese can be added on the top. Serve in shells with a sprinkling of chopped parsley.

Crab and Spinach Patties

Ingredients for 4

8 oz/½lb fresh crab meat
1lb/500g fresh spinach
One small onion, chopped
1 tablespoon lemon juice
1 beaten egg
2oz/60g cream cheese
A small pot single cream
Black pepper to taste
One large packet frozen puff pastry
Milk to glaze

Thaw the pastry. Wash and cook the spinach, leaving it quite firm. Drain thoroughly and leave to cool in the colander. In the meantime pick the meat off the crab shell and claws. Combine crab meat with the chopped spinach, lemon juice, onion, pepper, cream cheese and grated cheese. Mix well.

Roll the pastry and divide in 4 squares. Divide the crab and spinach mixture in four portions and spoon on to each pastry square. Fold each corner of pastry towards the middle, seal well by pinching all sides making sure to leave a small hole in the middle for the steam. Glaze with milk and bake in a hot oven (425°F, 200°C, gas mark 7) until crisp and golden brown.

Just before serving, pour a small amount of cream previously warmed up into each patty.

Cromer dip

Ingredients for 4

8oz/250g fresh crab meat
Crab paste
1 large pot thick sour cream or creme fraiche
2 finely chopped spring onions
1 handful garlic chives or chives
1 tablespoon freshly squeezed lemon juice
½ teaspoon Cambridge sauce or Worcestershire sauce
Pepper or Cayenne pepper to taste

Combine all the ingredients and chill for a few hours. Serve as a first course or with drinks with crusty bread or Suffolk rusks (see recipe page 169)

Crabmeat ramequins

Ingredients for 4

8oz/250g fresh crab meat
8oz/250g cream cheese
3 tablespoons dry white wine
½ teaspoon creamed horseradish
1 tablespoon chopped chives and parsley
A dash of Worcestershire sauce

Preheat the oven to 400°F, 200°C gas mark 6

Mix the fresh crab meat with all the other ingredients. Divide into 4 ovenware ramequins. Bake in the warmed oven until bubbly and light brown. Serve with bread or Suffolk rusks (see recipe page 169).

LOBSTER

Sheringham is to lobster what Cromer is to crab and freshly boiled lobster can be purchased at fish stalls all along the Norfolk coast or at the major markets. Happily modern distribution systems mean that we can enjoy fresh Norfolk lobsters throughout most of Britain.

If you are ever on the A10, near Downham Market on a Saturday, turn off for the village of Stow Bardolph and stop at the Hare Arms, the village public house and restaurant on Sir Thomas Hare's estate. David McManus and his pretty wife Trish will prepare for you the most delicious lobster salad from a marvellous counter display of freshly cooked lobsters. Each one is weighed and priced – just make your choice and within minutes you will be enjoying a local speciality.

If, on the other hand you have decided to prepare your own lobster, it is worth taking time for a visit to the Colman's Mustard shop at 3 Bridewell Alley, Norwich. The herby dried mustards only available at the shop will add a delightful piquancy to any mayonnaise you would serve with the lobster or give the necessary subtle flavour to your lobster Thermidor.

Mayonnaise dressing for cold lobster

Much lighter than normal mayonnaise, this dressing is ideal with lobster salad. Make a large cup of mayonnaise with one egg yolk mixed with a good pinch of Colman's dry mustard with chives. Once the mayonnaise is finished, fold in the content of a small jar of sour cream, one tablespoon of fresh parsley, black pepper to taste and as much as you wish of the lobster coral. Serve chilled.

Lobster thermidor

Ingredients for the sauce

3½oz/100g butter
2oz/60g plain flour
½ pt/¼ litre milk
4oz/120g grated cheese
1 dessertspoon Colman's tarragon and thyme dry mustard
1 pinch Cayenne pepper
1 tablespoon very dry sherry
A few breadcrumbs

Preheat the oven to 425°F, 220°C, gas mark 7

Make the sauce: Stir butter and flour over low heat with a wooden spoon, add a little milk at a time, keeping the mixture very smooth. Add the grated cheese and mix well. Then add the mustard, cayenne pepper and sherry.

Take the meat from the freshly boiled lobster and cut it into bite-size cubes. Put the shell on to a baking tray and spoon some of the sauce into the shell. Now lay the lobster cubes and cover with the rest of the sauce. Sprinkle a few breadcrumbs on top and dot a little butter from place to place. Place in the oven for 15 minutes, or until the filling is hot and the topping is golden brown.

MUSSELS

The Brancaster to Blakeney coastline is the only EEC pollution free harbour in Britain. It was confirmed by Mervyn Nudds whose family business of mussel farming has been going on for some 200 years.

From his cottage, at Brancaster Staithe we walked to the 'fishermen's hard', the local name for the natural stretch of sand which harbours the small boats, huts and nets of all kinds.

The tools of the mussel farming trade are simple – a small locally built boat called a flat, a long handled net with a metal rake at the end called a dydle, large purse shaped nets with a simple curved wooden handle made during the winter's months and a small metal grader for the sizing of the mussels.

Mervyn Nudds will take off early in the morning from May onwards to fetch the mussel spawns from the sandbanks and bring them back to the holding pits where they will be layed 'like any other crop' he said, and left to fatten in the clear water.

'Mussels were only used as bait in the old days. It is now such a delicacy, so much in demand by the British public' said Mr Nudds 'that I produce two to three tonnes a week single handed'.

His wife, Ann, who runs a local restaurant with a friend sat with me to discuss and exchange a few recipes. . .

Mussels in their own liquid

Clean the mussels, discard the beard and place them in a deep saucepan with a very small amount of water. Cover the pan, bring to the boil and, shaking the pan from time to time, cook for a few minutes until they have all opened. Do not prolong the cooking or they would toughen. Take the mussels out of their shells and eat them warm or cold with bread and butter, a little pepper, lemon juice or vinegar.

Mussels in white wine

Any of the East Anglian dry white wine would suit this recipe.

Ingredients for 4

2 pints mussels
Water
One large knob butter rolled in a little flour
One glass white wine
One onion
One small clove of garlic (optional)
Parsley, a sprig of thyme, one bayleaf
Black pepper

Clean the mussels, discard the beard. In a large stew pan pour a glass of water and the glass of white wine, add the onion and garlic finely chopped, the chopped parsley, thyme and bayleaf. Bring the mixture to the boil, add the black pepper and the mussels. Mix well with a wooden spoon, cover the pan and leave to cook for a few minutes until all the shells are opened. Transfer the mussels in their shells into a deep serving dish. Keep warm. Add butter to the stock, bring back to the boil reducing it slightly. Pour the sauce over the mussels and eat in individual soup plates, with plenty of crusty bread.

Mussel and shrimp potato dumplings in a white wine sauce

A lighter version of the traditional suet dumpling, a dish to serve in individual ovenproof dishes with a sprinkling of chervil and chives. Each dumpling should not be much larger than a bite size.

Ingredients for 4

1lb/500g potatoes
2 eggs
2oz/60g flour
Pepper to taste
A touch of mace
3 mussels and 3 shrimps per dumpling

For the sauce:
½ pt/¼ litre mussel stock
One small pot double cream
A handful chopped chervil and chives

Proceed as above (Mussels in white wine) to cook the mussels. Pick them out of the shells and reserve the stock to make the sauce. Peel the shrimps. Peel and boil the potatoes, mash them with the eggs, flour, pepper and mace. Leave to cool a little, then, roll in small balls. Push mussels and shrimps into each dumpling, making indentation with thumb. Reshape balls, roll in flour.

Bring a pan of water to the boil and lower the dumplings gently into the water. Poach them for 5 minutes. Drain well. Place them in the serving dishes.

Reduce the mussel stock to the desired thickness by boiling it. Remove the pan from the heat and whisk in the cream. Pour over the dumplings, bake in a very hot oven for a few minutes until sauce is hot. Sprinkle with herbs and serve immediately.

Soup of mussels and spring vegetables under a puff crust

A subtle mixture of tender East Anglian spring vegetables and mussels, sealed in individual dishes by a golden dome of puff pastry. It is absolutely necessary to clean the mussels thoroughly for this dish.

Ingredients for 4

One large packet frozen puff pastry
2 pints mussels
1 pint/½ litre water
1 small glass any East Anglian dry white wine
One bunch spring onions
2 baby turnips
4 small carrots
4 young leeks
Pepper to taste
1 tablespoon double cream
1 large knob butter
A bay leaf and a little dill

Wash, slice and cube all the vegetables and melt the butter in a large saucepan. As soon as the butter starts melting, stir in the sliced spring onions and cubed vegetables. Add water, white wine, herbs and pepper. Cover the pan and cook until the vegetables are just tender.

Clean the mussels, discarding the beard. Add them to the vegetable soup, cover and cook until all the shells are opened. Pick the mussels out of their shells and return mussels to the soup. Leave to cool. Preheat the oven to 425°F, 220°C, gas mark 7. Pour the cooled soup into 4 individual earthenware soup dishes, cover with the puff pastry and cook in the oven until golden and crisp.

COCKLES

Drive any time between 4 am and 10 am to Leigh-on-Sea in Essex, find your way to the cockle sheds and you can have the sea for breakfast. . . Thousands of the sweet shellfish are freshly boiled daily in the huts. Their taste when they just come out of the second boil has no parallel as I found out when I went to Mr Dell's shed one early spring morning.

The previous evening, standing on a dune of empty cockle shells – a sight to be seen for a start – I had watched a cockle boat being unloaded. Hanging the woven baskets on each end of the old wooden yolk they carry on their shoulders, the men were hurrying from the boat to the sheds. The only sound to be heard was the crackling of their gumboots on the shore and a few sandpipers fishing late on the mud of the Thames estuary . . . it could have been a hundred years back.

A few days later, armed with a rake and a sack, I made my way to Stiffkey in Norfolk and joined the local families raking the sand in search of the native blue shelled cockle – the 'Stiffkey blue'. It is not gathered commercially anymore, but, back home with my sea harvest, I experimented with a few recipes.

You can use any good cockles of course.

First, a quick delicious snack . . .

Cockles and watercress on a bed of mashed potatoes

Wash the cockles in plenty of water, many times, for they tend to be a little sandy. If you prefer, use freshly shelled cockles bought at the fishmonger's.

Ingredients for 4

1 pint cockles
2 spring onions
1 small bunch watercress, chopped
2oz/60g butter
1 teaspoon flour
A few drops anchovy essence
Black pepper to taste
1lb/500g potatoes

Put the cockles in a large saucepan with a small amount of water, cover the pan and cook until the shells open. Pick the cockles out of their shells and reserve the liquor for the sauce.

Make the sauce: melt the butter with flour, add the chopped watercress and spring onions. Stir well. Now add the cockles, their liquor, the pepper and anchovy essence. Cook for a few minutes until the sauce thickens. Boil and mash the potatoes and serve with the cockle sauce on top.

Cockles on horseback

This is particularly nice with streaky oak-smoked bacon to be found all over East Anglia. Skewer together a few cooked cockles rolled into a small piece of rindless streaky bacon. Fry gently in lard or bacon fat and serve, as a snack with drinks.

Essex chowder

Ingredients for 4

4 slices Essex oak smoked streaky bacon
4 medium new potatoes, diced
2 onions, chopped
4 tomatoes
A knob of butter
A handful chopped parsley or chervil
2 pints cockles in their shells
A large glass of Essex dry white wine
Water
Black or white pepper to taste

Fry the bacon in butter until crisp and set aside. Peel the tomatoes by dipping them for 5 minutes in hot water. Chop them roughly. Peel the potatoes and dice them. Saute potatoes, onions and tomatoes in the bacon fat. As soon as the onions are transparent, add the white wine, bring to the boil and transfer to a large saucepan. Cover with water, season with pepper and simmer until potatoes are tender.

In the meantime clean the cockles thoroughly. When the soup is nearly ready place the cockles in a saucepan with a little water, cover and cook until they open. Take them out of their shells and transfer the cockles and their liquor to the soup pan. Serve immediately topped with the bacon, chopped chervil or parsley.

WHELKS

'There is only one way to eat whelks' said a man on Norwich market 'Just plain boiled with salt, pepper and vinegar'. He was obviously a whelks connoisseur – I am not. But, after visiting Anne Woolfson who makes a natural flavoured, additive free mustard in Burnham-on-Crouch, I bought some whelks at the shellfish stall, and, using a few herbs from the garden and a leftover of East Anglian white wine I compiled the following recipe:

1 large teaspoon Burnham tomato mustard
1 tablespoon white wine
2 tablespoons oil
Freshly ground black pepper
1 teaspoon chopped chives
A little fresh coriander, chopped
A little fresh lovage, chopped

Remove the hard cover and tail of the whelks and slice them. Mix together the dressing ingredients, beating well with a fork. Pour over the whelks. Prepare a few hours in advance for the flavours to blend. Serve cold with crusty bread.

OYSTERS

In the year 50 B.C. an aloof Roman said: ' Poor Britons, there is some good in them after all, they produce the oyster'. That was in Camulodunum, the Roman name for Colchester. Today, the native flat oyster grown in the shallows around Mersea Island under the close supervision of Mr R.C. Kerrison is the object of a ceremony which takes place at the Moot Hall, Colchester, every last Friday in October.

The Colchester Oyster Feast is of very ancient origin and has been attended by a great number of dignitaries over the years including many members of the Royal Family. It is preceeded earlier in the year by the official opening of the Colne Fishery by the Mayor of Colchester. On the days of the Colchester Oyster Feast, some 2000 oysters are consumed in their raw state, served with a glass of draught Guinness.

Further up the coast, in Suffolk this time, Pacific oysters are to be found at the Butley-Orford Oysterage. They originate from a hatchery in north Kent and are laid to fatten in a pollution free creek just outside Orford under the careful attention of Richard Pinney. There is no season for the Pacific oyster. So, all year round, one can marvel at the freshness of the Orford oysters over a glass of local wine – they keep a few on their wine list.

Finally to the north Norfolk coast where at Sealdbeck Barn, Morston, one can purchase Pacific oysters from Major Athill, a retired army officer, the official warden for the National Trust of the Morston marshes. From the exquisite chintzy comfort of his sitting room, with commanding views of the salt marshes and the distant sea from every window, Major Athill described his total involvement with his stretch of the Norfolk coast and its products. As well as the farming of oysters in the non polluted waters of the Blakeney harbour, Major Athill finds joy in fishing for whitebait, grey mullet, sea trout, brill and dabs. Joined by his wife Mary who makes a deliciously fiery ginger cake, we discussed the many uses of oysters in the English cuisine.

Just from reading Charles Dickens one realises that the oyster used to play a great part in the diet of the British. It would seem that most of the cooked oyster recipes originate from East Anglia.

Oyster loaf

The oyster loaf was served for breakfast in the local inns. The recipe travelled with the first settlers to America where its more up to date version is still to be found:

Ingredients for 4

4 individual cottage loaves
16 oysters
One clove of garlic
3oz/90g butter
½ teaspoon white pepper
A few drops anchovy essence
A pinch of ground mace

Preheat the oven to 375°F, 190°C, gas mark 5

Take the tops off each cottage loaf and carefully scoop out the crumbs. Peel the clove of garlic, slice it in half and rub the garlic inside the bread. Open the oysters and empty their contents with the liquid in a pan. Add the butter and other ingredients and simmer, uncovered until slightly reduced. Fill each bread loaf with the oyster mixture, replace the tops and put in the warmed oven until warmed through.

Oysters on horseback

Ingredients for 4

4 slices brown bread
8 oysters
8 slices oak smoked streaky bacon
A little lard
Black pepper to taste

Open the oysters, detach them from their shell and pat them dry. Cut the rind off the bacon and fry gently in a little lard until just transparent. Cut 4 circles of bread and fry in the bacon fat. Roll each oyster in a slice of bacon, secure with a skewer, fry quickly on all sides and serve on the fried bread.

Mr Kerrison's oyster ramequins

1 pint oysters, minced
4 egg yolks
4 tablespoons double cream
Cayenne pepper to taste

In a basin beat the egg yolks, add the minced oysters, pepper, cream and a tablespoon of oyster juice. Pour into individual ramequins and cook in a bain-marie at 350°F, 180°C, gas mark 4 for 20 minutes. Serve with toast.

Oysters baked with herbs

Ingredients for 4

24 oysters
30g/1oz butter
3 spring onions or shallots
One bunch watercress
A handful of parsley
3 soupspoons chopped fennel leaves
1 tablespoon double cream
5 tablespoons breadcrumbs
Cayenne pepper to taste

Open the oysters and drain them in a colander. Wash and keep the shallow shell. Clean the watercress and chop the leaves together with the parsley and fennel leaves. Melt half the butter in a pan and simmer the herb mixture in it for five minutes. Add the Cayenne pepper and cream and mix well.

Return the oysters to their shells and spoon the herb mixture over each one. Melt the remaining butter and quickly stir in the breadcrumbs. Sprinkle over each oyster and bake in a hot oven 425°F, 220°C, gas mark 7 for six to ten minutes. Serve with crusty bread.

Oyster stuffing for turkey

Ingredients

6 oysters, drained and chopped
6 slices of bread made into fresh breadcrumbs
One onion, chopped
2 sticks celery, chopped
2oz/60g butter
3 tablespoons chopped parsley
1 tablespoon thyme
½ teaspoon chopped sage
1 teaspoon marjoram
½ teaspoon oregano
1 egg
Pepper

Melt the butter in a frying pan. Add the onion and celery, cook until transparent. Add the breadcrumbs and the remaining ingredients, including the chopped oysters. Mix well. Leave in a cool place for a few hours for the flavours to blend before cooking the turkey.

SHRIMPS

John Williamson of Kings Lynn has been fishing the Wash all the way to Skegness for the sweet pink and brown shrimps for 22 years. What started as a one man-one boat business has now turned into a prolific industry. For the Kings Lynn shrimp is in great demand not only in East Anglia but also in other parts of the country. The little pink shrimp, like a miniature prawn, is succulent and as I mention samphire later on I would like to let you share one of my favourite sandwiches: a unique taste of East Anglia.

Shrimp and samphire sandwich

Most people eat samphire boiled or steamed but, having picked some in the pollution free waters of Brancaster I wanted to taste it raw. Allow a stem of samphire per sandwich, some unsalted butter on thinly sliced wholemeal or granary bread, lemon juice and black pepper. Peel the shrimps, wash the samphire carefully, detach the tips from the stem and pile with the shrimps in between two slices of lightly buttered bread, sprinkle pepper over it and add a squeeze of lemon juice.

Potted shrimps and asparagus on toast

A delicious lunchtime snack

This recipe was born after purchasing the delicious potted shrimps, free of additives or colouring but full of taste, prepared by Susie Rhodes at the Cley Smoke House at Cley-next-the-sea, Norfolk. Combined with the delicate flavour of the small green Norfolk asparagus, they make a delightful snack.

Ingredients for 4

4 slices brown bread	**A dozen asparagus**
4 jars potted shrimps	

Wash, boil and drain the asparagus. Reheat the potted shrimps. Toast the bread on both sides. Lay the asparagus over the bread and top each toast with the shrimps in their spicy butter.

Shrimp dip

Ingredients

8oz/250g shrimps, peeled	**One small onion, chopped**
2 teaspoons chopped parsley	**1 teaspoon chopped chives**
8oz/250g cream cheese	**1 teaspoon Worcestershire sauce**
2 tablespoons mayonnaise	**A pinch of Cayenne pepper**

Mix all the ingredients. Chill for several hours, serve with Suffolk rusks (see recipe page 169)

SAMPHIRE

This delicate marshplant with its pungent taste of the sea is becoming very fashionable all over Britain. But for Pat Clarke of Castle Acre, it is not a novelty – it is the summer delicacy he has been eating all his life. On a grey January day, sitting around the huge inglenook fireplace at the local pub, The Ostrich, we were all complaining about the effects of the cold weather on our aches and pains when Ivan said 'Never mind Pat, it will soon be the samphire season'. Pat's eyes sparkled and I learnt everything I wanted to know about the sea vegetable during the conversation which followed.

In north Norfolk, where most of it is to be found, the samphire is washed, boiled and eaten with melted butter, black pepper and sometimes a few drops of vinegar. I also learnt that although it is supposed to be in season from June to September, the first stems are really the tender ones and as far as the Norfolk people are concerned, the season only lasts two to three weeks at the most. It is then that I tasted it raw in a sandwich (see page 28); it was a delight.

I also realised that it can be used in many dishes as a summer herb to enhance a fish or shellfish dish, or even in a sauce when pickled for, once preserved, it makes a delicious condiment to be used during the winter months.

Samphire – the asparagus of the sea

1lb/500g samphire

For the melted butter
4oz/120g butter
Plenty of freshly ground black pepper
A few drops of lemon juice

Wash the samphire in plenty of water. Boil for a few minutes. Drain and serve immediately with the lemon butter, detaching the tips with a fork.

Samphire – the gherkin of the sea

(An old recipe from the Benns family, corn and seed merchants at Great Yarmouth.)

Wash the samphire and pat it dry with a tea towel. Place in layers in a mixing jar with sea salt. Leave in a cool place until the following day. Rinse and pat dry again. Place it in a pan and cover with a good pickling vinegar. Bring to the boil and immediately transfer into pickling jars with a few peppercorns. Seal the jars and leave in a cool place for at least three weeks.

Samphire, crab and codling soup

Ingredients for 4

One small codling
One good size crab
½ lb/250g fresh samphire
One carrot
2 spring onions
1 teaspoon tomato puree
1 bay leaf
A small glass of East Anglian white wine
Pepper to taste

Place fish in a large saucepan, cover with water and the glass of wine, add the sliced carrot, spring onion and bay leaf. Simmer gently until the fish is flaky. Remove bayleaf.

In the meantime, wash the samphire. Pick crabmeat from the shell and claws, reserving the paste. Mix the paste with tomato puree. Lift the fish from stock. Remove head, bones and trimmings. Skin and cut into chunks. Bring the stock to the boil adding more water if necessary. Cook the samphire in the stock leaving it quite crisp. Using a fork, remove the stems. Return the tips to the soup and add crabmeat and fish. Simmer for a few minutes until the crabmeat is warmed through. Add the paste, stir in and serve with croutons or warm bread.

East Anglia seafood salad

This salad is a mixture of any of the East Anglian shellfish you can find i.e. cockles, shrimps, cooked mussels, crab, lobster – and of course samphire. Boil the samphire leaving it quite crisp. Remove the stems. Leave to cool completely. Have all the shellfish cooked, cold and off their shells.

for the dressing you will need:

2 tablespoons oil	**Chives, parsley, spring onion**
½ the juice of a lemon	**Black pepper to taste**

Mix the dressing ingredients together with a fork, beating well. Fold in the shellfish, check the seasoning and serve cold with brown bread and a garnish of lettuce and any salad vegetable you choose to have.

Fish

Fish

With over 300 miles of East Anglian coastline, fish plays a vital role in the economy of the region as well as in its cuisine. The fishing industry is dominated by the fish markets at Grimsby and Lowestoft, where ton after ton of countless varieties of North Sea fish are auctioned daily, but most port and resorts have their own small fleet of fishing boats to add to the variety.

According to the season, each area specialises in one type of fish: Dover sole, plaice and sea bass from April to October off the Essex and Suffolk coast, followed by herring, cod and whiting from October onwards. Dabs, flounders whitebait and sea trout will be brought to shore at Southwold and Walberswick while, weather permitting, the Alderburgh fishermen will slide their boats down the shingled beach for their autumn and winter catch of sprats.

Skate will be found off the Norfolk coast together with grey mullet, witch sole, a cross between a dab and a lemon sole, rock fish, conger, monkfish, turbot, halibut and of course winter herring 'piloted' by the handsome long nosed garfish.

And then there are eel, perch and other varieties of freshwater fish from the Fens and the Norfolk broads and delicious trout farmed and smoked all over the region.

The dry fruity East Anglian wine is the ideal drink with such fish and in many cases can be added to the cooking or the sauce to create a dish of distinctive flavour. In some cases, the rose wine can also be used.

SEA FISH

Devilled Herrings

Ingredients for 4

4 herrings
White flour
2 egg whites
2 dessertspoons white wine mustard
4oz/120g fresh breadcrumbs
3oz/90g butter
Salt and pepper to taste
A cupful of fresh chopped chives

Preheat the oven to 450°F, 230°C, gas mark 8. Melt 1 oz of butter over low heat. Clean the fish, pat dry with kitchen towel and roll it in flour. Start whisking the egg whites until quite stiff and fold in the mustard, a little at a time. Dip the floured fish in this mixture, then sprinkle with the fresh breadcrumbs. Place the fish in a baking dish and pour half of the melted butter over it. Season with salt and pepper. Bake in oven for twenty minutes, basting the fish once or twice. Serve with melted butter and chopped chives.

SPRATS

On a crisp November morning I made my way to Aldeburgh, timeless sea resort of the Suffolk coast. The serene grey sea frothed rhythmically on the shingle and I could see that the catch had been good. I had a chat with William Burrell, known locally as Billy, and bought some fresh sprats. 'Not so much in demand these days' he said. What a pity. They are so delicious.

Clutching an old family recipe, I rushed home to prepare soused sprats. There are many ways of preparing soused or 'potted' sprats as they are known locally. This herby recipe is delicious and will keep well in a cold room. An easy first course or snack with bread, butter and a glass of wine. . .

Aldeburgh potted Sprats

Ingredients for 2lbs/1kg of sprats

2lbs/1kg fresh sprats	**2 bayleaves**
1 pt/½ litre vinegar	**2 onions**
1 pt/½ litre dry white wine	**2 cloves**
A few sprigs of parsley	**A few black peppercorns, crushed**
A little tarragon	**1 clove of garlic**
Thyme	**2 small carrots**

Pour the vinegar and white wine in a deep pan, add parsley, tarragon thyme and bayleaves, garlic, cloves and the black pepper. Bring to the boil, then simmer until the liquid reduces by half. Clean the sprats, pat them dry and lay them at the bottom of a glass or earthenware jar on a bed of sliced carrots and onions. Leave a good inch between the fish and the top of the jar. Pour the boiling liquid over the fish, cover and leave in a cold room for at least 3 days before eating.

Barbecued Sprats

Fresh sprats are wonderful cooked over a fire.

Clean them well, fasten them in rows by running a skewer through their gills, place them over the hot charcoal embers and grill until nicely brown. Eat with lemon juice or a few drops of vinegar, bread and butter.

WHITING

When we lived in Suffolk, I used to get masses of freshly caught whiting from our neighbour who fished off the Orford coast at weekends. Here are a few of my recipes.

Whiting in foil

An unusual combination of fish and grated cheese, a very mild dish to have with boiled or mashed potatoes.

Ingredients for 4

4 whiting fillets
2 tablespoons chopped parsley
1 small onion, chopped finely
4oz/120g grated cheese
4 wooden skewers
4 rectangles of foil
Salt and pepper to taste

Preheat the oven to 425°F, 220°C, gas mark 7

Season the whiting fillets. With a fork mix together the grated cheese, chopped parsley and finely chopped onion. Spoon the mixture over the fish and roll each fillet carefully onto itself. Secure with a wooden skewer. Wrap in foil and bake in the oven for 20 minutes.

Baked Whiting fillets with mushrooms and tomatoes

Ingredients for 4

4 whiting fillets
½lb/250g small mushrooms, sliced
1 onion
4 tomatoes
Mixed herbs of your choice
1 tablespoon white wine (optional)
1oz/30g butter

Preheat the oven to 425°F, 220°C, gas mark 7.

Lay the sliced onion at the bottom of a buttered dish together with the sliced mushrooms. Lay the fish fillet on top. Dot with butter and cook in the preheated oven for 10 minutes or until the butter starts browning. Slice the tomatoes, remove the seeds and lay the slices on top of the fish. Sprinkle with the mixed herbs, baste with the cooking juices and return to the oven for a further 5 minutes. Now add the wine and replace in oven for a further 8 minutes. Serve from the dish with boiled potatoes.

Whiting with a mushroom, lovage and lemon balm stuffing

Fresh herbs are grown a great deal in large varieties in East Anglia. The slight celery flavour of the lovage with the sharp bite of the lemon balm give this dish a very distinctive flavour. Use a very small amount of the balm for it is very pungent.

Ingredients for 4

4 good size whiting
2oz/60g button mushrooms
2 lovage leaves
½ lemon balm leaf
1 tablespoon fresh breadcrumbs
White pepper to taste
2oz/60g melted butter
3 tablespoons double cream
1 tablespoon dry white wine

Preheat the oven at 425°F, 220°C, gas mark 7.

Melt the butter over low heat. Chop the mushrooms with the lovage and lemon balm. Combine half of the melted butter with herbs and pepper. Spoon the stuffing inside each fish. Lay in a baking dish, pour the rest of the melted butter over the fish and bake for 25 minutes or until the fish is flaky. Mix the cream with the white wine, pour over the fish and return to the oven for a further 6 minutes until the cream starts bubbling. Serve at once.

SKATE

This firm mild fish is caught off the East Anglian coast from Grimsby to Essex. At Burnham-on-Crouch I spoke to Ray Hawkins who turned a schoolboy hobby into a job and has been fishing off the Thames estuary for the last 20 years. Dover sole is his main business but 'when I catch skate' he added 'we always use my mother's recipe!'

Joyce Hawkins's Skate in parsley sauce

Ingredients for 4

2 large skate wings
1 pt/½ litre milk

For the sauce
1 handful chopped parsley
1 dessertspoon flour
A large knob of butter
Salt and pepper to taste

Preheat the oven to 400°F, 200°C, gas mark 6.

Place the fish in a large baking dish, cover with the milk, salt and pepper and bake until flaky. Lift the fish off the stock, skin it and keep warm while you make the sauce. Melt the butter and add the flour, stirring constantly with a wooden spatula. Slowly add the fish liquor and stir until the sauce thickens. Then add the chopped parsley. Pour the sauce over the fish and serve with peeled, boiled new potatoes.

Skate in a pink sauce

The rose wine of East Anglia is an excellent addition to this sauce, very smooth and very special.

Ingredients for 4

2 large skate wings
1 bayleaf
1 sprig of thyme
Salt and freshly ground black pepper

For the sauce:
6 oz/180g butter
2 glasses East Anglian rose wine
2 chopped shallots
A touch of tomato puree
A pinch of paprika
1 small pot of thick cream

Place the fish in a deep pan, cover with water, add thyme, bayleaf, salt and pepper. Bring to the boil, lower the heat immediately and leave it to simmer until white and flaky. Lift from the stock, remove the skin and keep the fish warm on a serving dish.

Just before the end of cooking of the skate, start making the sauce: Pour the wine in a small saucepan and add the chopped shallots. Bring to the boil and reduce until the wine has almost disappeared. Add the cream, stir well. Strain through nylon sieve to remove shallot. Now, whisk in the butter in small pieces over the lowest heat possible. The sauce should be very smooth. Add the tomato paste and paprika. Pour over the fish and serve at once.

Skate with parsley and watercress

Watercress used in small quantity not only gives a bite but also enhances the flavour of certain fish and shellfish. Certainly it is the case with skate.

Ingredients for 4

2 large skate wings
1 bayleaf
1 sprig of thyme
A few sprigs of watercress, chopped
A few sprigs of parsley, chopped
2oz/60g butter
Salt and pepper to taste

Place the fish in a large saucepan with the bayleaf, thyme, salt and pepper. Cover with water, bring to the boil and, reducing the heat, simmer until white and flaky.

Melt the butter over low heat, add the parsley and watercress and simmer for a few minutes.

Lift the fish from the stock and, after removing the skin, serve with the herby butter and new potatoes.

CONGER

Conger Eel with bacon and hot peas

I once made a voyage of discovery to Norwich market under the implicit instruction from a neighbour that I had to try the 'green peas in their own liquid'. I obediently made my way through the maze of colourful stalls, following the 'hot peas' signs pointing eventually towards Reggie's pea stall 'established 35 years'. I had obviously stumbled over the reputable place. There were lots of cooked peas and also gravyboats full of mint sauce. I paid for a portion and watched the family standing by me. It was simple, spoon a little mint sauce over the peas and eat with a spoon. Result: ambrosia. And certainly more healthy than the greasy onions floating in a pan at the next stall!

I have since then cooked my own peas in their own liquid. They may not be as nice as Reggie's but they make a pretty good accompaniment for a piece of conger eel. I prepare this dish when our garden peas are past their best and have turned large and very mealy.

Ingredients for 4

2lbs/1kg middle cut of conger eel	**6 to 8 pickling onions**
6 slices Norfolk sweet cured bacon	**A knob of butter**
2lbs/1kg large peas	**Pepper to taste**
1 small glass of East Anglian dry white wine	

Ask your fishmonger to skin the fish. Wrap the whole piece with the bacon slices and secure with string or a wooden skewer.

Preheat the oven to 425°F, 220°C, gas mark 7

Place the fish in a baking dish, season with pepper, add the knob of butter on the top, the peeled onions around the fish and cook in the oven for 40 minutes. In the meantime, shell the peas and cook them with a little water and salt in a covered saucepan. They should be covered with just enough liquid not to dry. Five minutes before serving the fish, add the white wine to the stock, baste the fish and return to oven. Slice the fish, and serve with peas and cooking juices.

COD

I watched the men filleting cod at Grimsby. It is done with such dexterity. All on perfectly clean wooden slabs, constantly awash with running water. They skin, fillet and slice for cod steaks, but the small round cod cheeks will be kept separately. They are the filleters' perks. They will tell you it is the sweetest part of the fish. Cod cheeks can be purchased at reputable fishmonger's and are indeed a real delicacy.

The filleters hot pot

Ingredients for 4

1lb/500g cod cheeks	**½ pt/¼ litre milk**
2oz/60g butter	**1 bayleaf**
1 carrot	**2 large potatoes**
1 onion	**Black pepper and salt to taste**
1 stick of celery	**1 tablespoon flour**
1 handful of shelled peas	**A few drops anchovy essence**

Roll the cod cheeks in flour. In a deep pan melt 1oz/30g of butter and quickly fry the fish until lightly browned. Add the milk, the carrots sliced, the celery chopped, the peas, the onion and bayleaf. Cover the pan partially and simmer until fish and vegetables are tender. Check the seasoning, add the anchovy essence. In the meantime peel and boil the potatoes, leaving them quite firm. Preheat the oven to very hot (475°F, 240°C, gas mark 9)

Transfer the fish stew into an ovenproof dish, slice the potatoes and arrange them neatly over the fish. Melt the rest of the butter and pour over the potatoes. Place in oven for 15 minutes or until the potatoes are crisp and golden brown. Serve at once.

Cod cheeks in a fresh tarragon and mustard sauce

Ingredients for 4

16 cod cheeks	**1 dessertspoon mustard**
2 lemons	**A few tarragon leaves**
2oz/60g butter	**1 tablespoon flour**
2 dessertspoons thick cream	**Salt and pepper to taste**

Roll the cod cheeks, one by one in the flour. Melt the butter in a frying pan. As soon as it bubbles stir in the fish, turning from time to time until golden brown. Season with salt and pepper. Transfer the fish onto a serving dish and make the sauce. Squeeze the juice of one lemon and add it to the cooking juices in the frying pan. Add the cream, the mustard and the chopped tarragon leaves. At the first bubble, pour the sauce over the fish and serve immediately with slices of fresh lemon.

The fisherman's stew

I serve this copious and nourishing dish as a one course meal with potatoes, followed by fruit or a light dessert. Serve it in individual large earthenware dishes which will accommodate the fish stew and the sizzling cheesy piece of toast on top.

Ingredients for 4 to 6

2lbs/1kg of any white fish – mixed
½ bottle of dry East Anglian white wine
3½oz/100g grated cheese
1 large onion
3 leeks
1 carrot
2 sticks of celery
A bunch of chervil, parsley and chives
1 sprig of fresh coriander
1 bayleaf
2 cloves
4 to 6 slices of bread
Salt and pepper to taste

Clean the fish and cut it in thick chunks. Wash and slice the vegetables. Insert cloves in the onion. Place fish, vegetables and herbs in a large stewpan. Add the wine and enough water to cover. Bring to the boil and lowering the heat, simmer gently for 20 minutes until fish and vegetables are cooked. Toast the bread on one side. Divide the stew in individual dishes adding plenty of stock to each one. Place the bread on its toasted side on each portion, sprinkle with greated cheese and place in a very hot oven or under the grill until the cheese is melting and starts to bubble. Serve with a dish of new potatoes to be dropped in the fish stew at everyone's convenience or appetite!

Sole, Lemon Sole, Dabs and Plaice

Although mainly fished along the coast of Essex, one can also buy them straight off the beach at Walberswick and Southwold, at the heart of Sole Bay. They are all so fine fleshed and tasty that it is really a shame to try too much with them.

At Southwold, last summer I bought little dabs on my way back from the beach and within one hour they were in the pan. What a joy!

Quick fried Dabs

Rub some flour on both sides of the fish. Heat up fresh vegetable oil. Dip the fish in the oil for a few minutes until golden brown and serve with quartered lemons, sea salt and black pepper.

Grilled Sole with pickled samphire butter

Pound together a few tips of pickled samphire with 2oz/60g of unsalted butter. Grill the sole and serve at once with the spiced butter.

Steamed Plaice or Lemon Sole with Lemon Butter

Steam or boil the fish and serve off the bone with a melted butter made with freshly ground sea salt and pepper and a large squeeze of lemon juice.

WHITEBAIT

The Whitebait Festival Story is best described by Keith Grant, General Secretary, Southend Chamber of Commerce:

Whitebait, the mixed fry of fish of all species has always been prolific in the Thames Estuary. Its annual day of glory was the Whitebait Feast, held till 1894 at Greenwich or Blackwall and traditionally attended by Cabinet Ministers and leading politicians. It marked the close of the Parliamentary session and was held on Trinity Monday (Whit Monday) or the nearest convenient day. It originated in Essex as a private dinner, annually enjoyed by some of the landed gentry who had been connected with the long and costly schemes to repair the great Thameside tidal inundation of 1707 known as the Dagenham Breach. The host, Sir Robert Preston, MP for Dover, invited distinguished guests either to the Breach House or to his 'Fishing Cottage' nearby. The Prime Minister, William Pitt the Younger, became a regular diner up to the time of his death, but asked for a venue closer to London. To suit him Greenwich was chosen and the local delicacy, whitebait, adopted.

The feast was revived in 1934 by Southend Chamber of Commerce Trade and Industry as part of a Whitebait Festival to take place in the Southend area. This opens with the Blessing of the Catch, with ministers of five denominations taking part in a ceremony which was held at the end of the famous Southend Pier till it was burnt down in 1976. After the blessing a whitebait lunch was served in the town, attended by the Mayor, MPs and other local dignitaries followed by a banquet in the evening to which well-known speakers were invited as well as the luncheon company. In 1974 it was recognised that two feasts in a day, even of whitebait, were taxing both appetites and purses. Moreover, it was difficult to attract speakers during September, the date when the blessing of the catch is always carried out, so the evening banquet was moved to October or November. In this form the Festival continues to the present day still organised by the Southend Chamber.

As the Southend Pier venue has not been available since 1976 the annual Blessing Ceremony and Luncheon has continued to take place in various locations situated in the Southend, Thorpe Bay and Leigh-on-Sea areas.

Fried Whitebait the old fashioned way

Wash the whitebait, drain in a colander and pat dry. Flour well. Beat some egg white, leaving it quite soft. Have some fine breadcrumbs ready. Dip the whitebait in the eggwhite, then sprinkle with breadcrumbs. Fry in hot lard, a small amount at a time. As soon as they

rise they are ready. Serve very hot with a sprinkling of freshly ground salt and finely chopped parsley.

Twice fried Whitebait

Have some very fresh oil ready in a pan equipped with a wire frying basket. Wash the whitebait, pat dry and roll in plenty of flour. As soon as the oil is ready, fill the basket with the fish and lower it in the oil for one minute. Lift it, let it rest for a while. Repeat the operation a second time. The whitebait stay crisp and fluffy that way. Serve piping hot with lemon quarters.

Pickled fried Whitebait

This makes an unusual cold first course to be served either with a potato salad or on its own with plenty of buttered brown bread.

Ingredients for a few jars

2lbs/1kg whitebait	**A pinch of Cayenne pepper**
2 large onions, sliced	**Pickling vinegar**
Thyme and bayleaf	**Pickling jars**
Peppercorns	**Plenty of flour**
A few cloves	**Frying oil**

Wash, drain and dry the whitebait. Roll in a generous amount of flour. Fry them in very hot oil for one minute, a small amount at a time. Drain well and season with salt. Slice the onions and blanch them for a few minutes in the pickling vinegar with the other ingredients. Leave to cool. When the fish and vinegar have cooled sufficiently, place whitebait in the pickling jars together with slices of onions, herbs and peppercorns. Seal the jars and keep in a cold place for at least 12 days before eating.

SMOKED SEA-FISH

Red Herrings and all that!

Red herrings. 'Yes they really do exist at Great Yarmouth': I began to wonder about the truth of it when I started on the trail, as recommended, of the fabled Bloater shop. The problem is that it does not bear that name any more. Finally I found it, and the red herrings, at Charles Eastick's smoke house, renamed the Fish shop in England Lane, Gorleston.

A retired fisherman, Charles Eastick known locally as Charlie now spends his days smoking fish as a one-man business. From the quality of the products, whether one chooses to buy kippers, strong-flavoured bloaters or red herrings I can well believe him when he says, 'Hundreds of people make a special trip to Yarmouth every year to buy the smoked fish'.

Further down the coast, at Lowestoft, I visited the smoke house of J. T. Cole's fish merchants. I was proudly shown round by Terry Jones, a young man who started by helping at the smoke house after school and is now in charge.

In the days when most of the so-called smoked products are just coloured and smoke flavoured I can very well understand the pride of the two men I visited. They are creating an excellent product, following an ancient tradition which, without people like them, would die. As you enter a smoke house the smell of the oak dust and the fish is enveloping and exquisite, and the sight extremely pleasing: row after row of freshly caught fish drying and tanning into a smoked delicacy. It's just mouthwatering.

Charles Eastick's way of cooking Red Herring

The red herring is salted for 48 hours and then kept for a minimum of 8 weeks at the very top of the smoke house. Once smoked it can then be kept for months. In East Anglia it is a winter delicacy, bought mainly from November onwards. 'Split it open, scald it in unsalted boiling water for a few minutes – the warmth of the water will draw up some of the salt and all the small bones of the fish. Remove the small bones and then put under the grill to finish cooking. Eat with bread and butter'.

Marinated kippers

This recipe has been written at the request of Robin Don, wine merchant and Master of Wine, owner of the Elmham Park vineyard.

Ingredients for 4 or more

8 kippers
1 pt/½ litre milk
A few celery leaves
3 large onions
A few sprigs of parsley
A few sprigs of thyme
6 juniper berries
Black peppercorns
½ bottle of East Anglian dry white wine
1 teaspoon wine vinegar
6 to 8 small pickled gherkins
One small carrot, finely sliced

Soak the kippers in milk for two hours. Pat them dry, split them in half and skin them. In an earthenware or glass jar, place a layer of kippers, a layer of the other ingredients, a layer of kippers. Pour the wine and vinegar over them. Seal the jar and leave to marinate in a cool place for four days. Eat as a first course with crusty bread and butter or with a warm potato salad.

The trawlerman's Kipper salad

Ingredients for 4

2 kippers
½ pt/¼ litre milk
4 tablespoons oil
1 herring soft roe, cooked
1 teaspoon strong mustard
1 glass of East Anglian white wine
White pepper to taste
1lb/500g potatoes
1 beetroot
1 small onion, chopped finely
Chopped chives and parsley to taste

Soak the kippers in milk for one hour. Pat them dry, skin and divide into fillets. Cover with 2 tablespoons of oil.

Make the dressing by mashing the cold soft roe with the mustard, mix with the other 2 tablespoons of oil, the white wine, the white pepper and the chopped onion, parsley and chives. Pour this dressing over a warm salad of freshly boiled potatoes and beetroot, and serve with the filleted kippers.

Other smoked fish products

And finally. . . while on the subject of smoked sea products I would like to mention that smoked cod and haddock as well as smoked roes and sprats can also be purchased at the places mentioned above.

Before I close this chapter, I certainly would like to say that if you are ever on the north Norfolk coast, stop at Cley-next-the-sea: with its huge windmill offering its sails to the wind of the salt marshes, its maze of cobbled flint cottages and the soft pastures at the back, Cley has kept the total charm of a small fishing town of yesteryear. There, from a tiny shop, Mike and Susie Rhodes run the Cley Smoke House. The display of home-prepared, colour and additive free products is very inviting. Susie Rhodes experiments constantly with new recipes. When I visited, she had just made a new herring pate which was as delicious as the herrings marinated in cider that I took home.

FRESHWATER FISH

EELS

For centuries, eels have been a great favourite in East Anglia, where they find their way from the Gulf Stream onto the backwaters of the Fens. And if 'pie and mash' and jellied eels are associated with the Saturday meals of East London Pearly Queens, the Fenland people still keep a fair share of the catch for their own table.

A man who knows a great deal about the fish and the way to catch it is 'Binks' Cottrell, head bailiff for the Cambridge division of Anglian Water. Under the tuition of a now retired eel catcher, Binks learnt the intricate art of making 'hives' and 'grigs' from locally grown willow – a fascinating form of basketry used to catch the fish. 'Nets are more commonly used these days' he said 'and I mostly make the originals for museums. East Anglia is the biggest eel fishing region in the U.K.' he added, 'and my wife Jo and I have spent the last 14 years experimenting with eel smoking, jellied eels and other recipes passed on by local catchers. My mother, Dorothy, cooks a splendidly rich eel stew!'

Mrs Cottrell's crocked Eels

Ingredients

2lbs/1kg eels
2oz/60g butter
1 medium size onion
1 dessertspoon chopped parsley
Salt and pepper

Skin and clean the fish. Cut in 2in pieces. Place in a stone jar, add butter, chopped onion and parsley, salt and pepper. Cover loosely. Place stone jar in a saucepan of cold water. Bring to the boil and cook until the eels are tender – about 1½ hours. When done, place eels on hot plate, pour a little gravy from the stone jar over them. Serve with home-made bread.

The Fenman's luncheon

Ingredients for 4

1½lb/750g eel, skinned and cut in large chunks
2 carrots, sliced
2 onions, chopped finely
1 egg
1 bayleaf
2 sprigs of thyme
2 sprigs of parsley
A few white peppercorns
A large cup of fine breadcrumbs
2 cloves
2oz/60g butter
½ a bottle of East Anglian white wine
1 teaspoon vinegar
Water

Pour the wine, vinegar and a little water in a large saucepan. Add the carrots, onions, herbs and spices. Bring to the boil, then lowering the heat simmer for 30 minutes. Now, place the pieces of fish in the stock, bring back to the boil, cover the pan and cook over a good heat for 30 minutes. Leave eel to cool in the stock until the following day. Then, lift the fish from the stock, pat as dry as possible. Beat the egg in one dish, place the breadcrumbs in another. Preheat the oven at 450°F, 230°C, gas mark 8.

Dip each piece of eel in the beaten egg, then roll in the breadcrumbs. Place into a baking dish, dot with a little butter and bake until warmed through and golden brown. Serve piping hot with the following sauce:

Ingredients for the sauce

4oz/120g mayonnaise
4oz/120g sour cream
1 tablespoon chopped parsley
4 finely chopped spring onions
1 teaspoon of horseradish
¼ teaspoon of dill
Salt and pepper to taste

Mix all the ingredients together with a fork. Chill before serving.

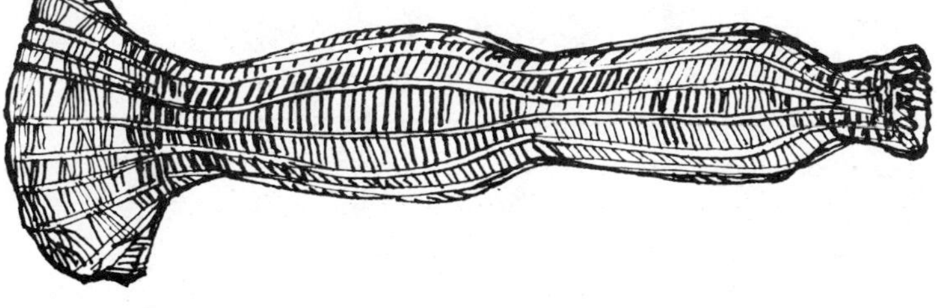

Eel stewed in white wine with garlic fried bread

Ingredients for 4

2lbs/1kg eel, skinned and cut in large chunks
½ bottle of fruity East Anglian white wine
½ bottle water
½lb/500g peeled small pickling onions
A bunch of herbs
1 carrot, sliced
A few white peppercorns
2oz/60g butter
1 tablespoon double cream
½ tablespoon mild mustard
1 dessertspoon flour
1oz butter
Salt

In a heavy saucepan, melt the 2oz of butter and add the flour stirring well. Now add the wine and water, a little at a time, stirring constantly to avoid lumps. Bring to the boil for 5 minutes. Lower in the pieces of fish, onions, carrot, peppercorns and salt, the bunch of herbs. Cover the pan and simmer for 30 minutes or until the fish feels tender and onions are cooked. Lift the fish from the pan and transfer onto a serving dish. Keep warm.

Make the sauce by bringing the stock to the boil, until the liquid reduces by half and then add the cream and mustard mixed, followed by the butter, little by little. The sauce should coat the back of a spoon. Pour the sauce over the fish. Serve with bread fried in garlic butter.

TROUT

Trout with hazelnut butter

An excellent way of preparing a freshly fished trout. Poached in herby wine stock with juniper berries, it is served with hazelnut butter.

Ingredients

The fish
1 glass East Anglian fruity white wine
Water
A bunch of herbs
6 juniper berries
6 black peppercorns
6 white peppercorns
Salt

Place the fish and other ingredients in a large pan or fish-kettle. Add enough water to cover. Bring to the boil and immediately reduce the heat so that the liquid just simmers for 20 minutes or so, according to the size of the fish. Serve straight off the stock with melted hazelnut butter.

To make hazelnut butter: You will need 5 large hazelnuts for every 1oz/30g of butter. Grind the hazelnuts, mix them with the butter, add salt and pepper and a squeeze of lemon juice to taste.

Ramequins of potted Trout with raspberry sauce

The delicate flavour of the cold fish and the fruity tang of the raspberry are a special taste sensation. Steam or boil the fish with a little dill and parsley. Let it cool. When cold, remove skin, bones and trimmings. Pound the flesh with a fork adding a small amount of lemony melted butter – just enough to bind it together. Divide into individual buttered ramequins. Chill overnight. Before serving, place the ramequins in warm water for a few seconds. Turn on to small plates.

To make the sauce: crush 6 fresh raspberries with 1 teaspoon of lemon juice and whisk in 2 dessertspoons of oil. Add salt and pepper to taste. Spoon a ribbon of sauce over each trout mould. Decorate with dill. Serve with brown bread.

SMOKED RIVER FISH AND FARMED FISH

Although the quality of farmed freshwater fish as against the taste of wild fish is arguable, fish farming is becoming more and more popular throughout the country. The methods and conditions under which the fish are reared are constantly supervised and there are some excellent species of farmed fish to be found. The recipes provided previously for freshwater fish can be used for any farmed fish, but I would like to conclude this chapter with a few words and ideas on smoked freshwater fish.

In each of the counties' reputable fish farms, excellent smoked trout can be purchased. And together with smoked eels and smoked salmon, they certainly provide the basis of good first or main courses.

Smoked Trout and horseradish dip

I made this dip with the creamed horseradish I bought at The Burnham Mustard Company, at Burnham-on-Crouch. Anne Woolfson mixes the freshly grated horseradish with local cream. The shelf life of this product is limited but it is so succulent it is well worth a trip or an order.

Ingredients

1 large smoked trout, skinned
8oz/250g thick cream
1 teaspoon horseradish
1 spring onion, chopped finely
1 teaspoon chopped chives
½ teaspoon Worcestershire sauce
Pinch of Cayenne pepper
Salt to taste
1oz/30g melted butter

Using a food processor, blend all the ingredients together. Chill, serve with brown bread or Suffolk rusks (see recipe page 169)

Smoked Trout and fresh samphire quiche

Ingredients for 4

Shortcrust pastry
2 spring onions, chopped
2oz/60g unsalted butter
1 large smoked trout, skinned
2 handful samphire tips
3 eggs
1 small jar double cream
½ teaspoon tomato puree
2oz/60g grated cheese

Preheat oven to 400°F, 200°C, gas mark 6.

Blanch the samphire. Drain well and pat dry. Saute spring onions in butter, add the trout in small chunks, add the samphire and set aside. Roll the pastry into a tart dish. Beat the eggs until fluffy, add cream and tomato puree. Fold in the trout and samphire mixture. Sprinkle with grated cheese. Bake 30 to 40 minutes. Serve immediately.

Breakfast of smoked trout and poached egg

A mild and unusual breakfast. Ask your fishmonger or trout farmer to fillet the smoked fish. Gently fry the fillets in unsalted butter. Serve with a poached egg, lemon juice and toasted brown bread.

Medley of river fish supreme

A mixture of smoked and unsmoked freshwater fish in a smooth white wine sauce. I recommend this dish for a very special luncheon or dinner party. It is quite easy to prepare, very unusual and excellent served with garlicky fried bread. It can be a nourishing winter first course or, served with new potatoes, followed by a tossed green salad of lettuce, watercress and spring onions, it makes then a delicious main course.

A good stock will be the key to a successful sauce. So, ask your fishmonger or trout farmer, when he fillets the fish to keep bones and trimmings for the stock.

Ingredients for 4

3 trout, fresh, filleted
1 large trout, smoked, filleted
8oz/250g smoked eel
4oz/120g smoked salmon

For the stock
2 onions
1 slice lemon
1¼ pt/¾ litre water
1 large glass East Anglian white wine
1 carrot, sliced
1 bayleaf
1 sprig of thyme
Freshly ground sea salt and black pepper
Fish bones, heads and tails

For the sauce
3oz/90g unsalted butter
2 large glasses fish stock
1 large glass East Anglian dry white wine
1 small glass dry vermouth
2 shallots, chopped
4oz/120g thick double cream
Salt and pepper to taste
A little fresh or dried dill
A pinch of saffron

First, make the stock. Place all the ingredients in a large saucepan. Bring to the boil and, reducing the heat, simmer uncovered for 20 minutes. Sieve the stock removing all the ingredients. Keep in a cool place until use. Keep 2 glassfuls aside for the sauce.

Secondly, poach the fish: Pour the remaining fish stock in a large pan. Bring to boiling point and gently place the mixed fish fillets in the liquid. Cover and, lowering the heat to a pip, cook for a maximum of 8 minutes.

In the meantime, make the sauce: Place chopped shallots, white wine, vermouth and fish stock in a saucepan and cook, uncovered, until the liquid reduced by half. Strain the liquid through a nylon sieve, return to pan and add the cream. Whisk in the butter, little by little over very low heat – at no time should the butter separate from the sauce.

Transfer the fish to individual plates. Cover with sauce, decorate with dill.

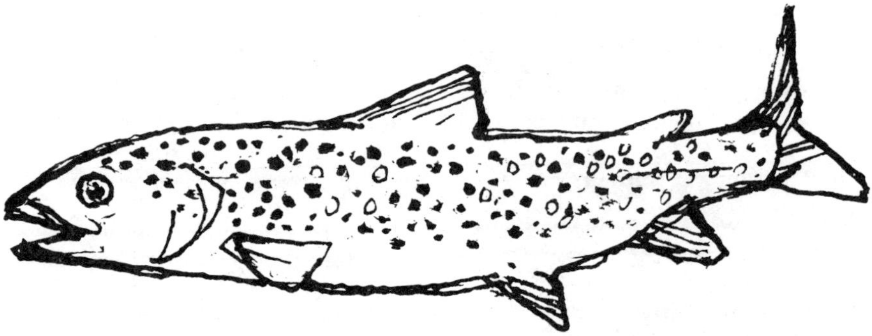

Game

Game

Without the Romans, who introduced the pheasant as an ornamental bird, the resources of East Anglian wildlife would not be the same. Without rabbit and hare thriving on farmland, a great deal of the rural population of East Anglia would, at one time, have been near to starvation. When one reads the history of the Breckland, rabbit, known then as 'hollow meat', was the staple diet of the poor. Fortunately those days are well behind us now, but the cooking of game is still very much an East Anglian tradition, as I found in the family scrap books lent to me.

The rearing of pheasant and partridge is under the constant control of knowledgeable landowners and their gamekeepers. The rules are strict and it is probably why, unlike the Continent where game resources have been so depleted by over-shooting, game is still so prolific in East Anglia.

In Norfolk, I visited Colin Dickerson, game dealer and fellow columnist. He writes for *Shooting Times* and *Shooting News*. The Dickersons have been game dealers since 1914 and throughout the year every species of game is available from their premises in Swaffham. They export a great deal to other parts of the country and abroad, but their door is always open, even on Sunday mornings, for local people to come and purchase game or wildfowl according to the season.

'Most people make the mistake of thinking that autumn and winter are the only two game seasons' said Colin Dickerson. 'I am always stressing the point that it is not so. For example venison can be found all year round and spring is an excellent season for pigeon'. He added: 'Game is good, lean and certainly one of the purest form of additive-free meat you can buy'.

Well, with so much to choose from – pheasant, partridge, wild duck, woodcock, pigeon, hare and rabbit – let's get on with some recipes.

Potted pigeon

Ingredients for 4

4 pigeon, cleaned and skinned
A pinch of thyme
A pinch of mace
A pinch of allspice
Plenty of freshly ground black pepper
Salt to taste
4oz/120g butter
1 glass of East Anglian white wine

With a fork, blend the spices into 2oz/60g of butter. Rub well over the birds. Lay the pigeons, breast down, in a casserole dish, packing them tightly together. Pour wine over them, cover and braise in a very low oven until the meat falls off the bones. Remove bones, cut the meat in small pieces adding whatever stock is left. Press down into jars. Cover each jar with melted butter and keep in a cool place.

Sauteed pigeon breasts

Ingredients for 4

8 pigeon breasts
2oz/60g butter
1 onion, chopped
2 sticks celery, chopped
2 sprigs tarragon
1 garlic clove
1 large glass of white wine
salt and pepper to taste

Saute the pigeons breasts one by one until golden brown. Add wine, onion, garlic, celery. Cover and simmer over low heat for 20 minutes. Add tarragon and simmer, uncovered, for a further 15 minutes. Serve with pan juices.

Pigeon and parsnip casserole

A delicious mixture of two very East Anglian products. The parsnips must be young and small. They will add a slightly smoky flavour to the dish.

Ingredients for 4

4 pigeons	**2oz/60g butter**
2 onions	**1 dessertspoon of flour**
2 small parsnips	**A bunch of herbs**
4oz/120g unsmoked streaky bacon	**Salt and pepper to taste**

Blanch the parsnips in salted water for a few minutes. Drain but keep the water. Saute the pigeons in butter on all sides until golden brown. Add the bacon cut in chunks and the onions. Sprinkle with flour. Mix well, add parsnip cooking stock and parsnips, cut in thick slices. Season, add herbs, cover and cook over low heat until tender. Serve with boiled potatoes and a green vegetable.

Partridge and cabbage casserole

(Recipe from Mrs K. Porter – The Roydon Cookery Book)

Ingredients

Brace of birds	**1 Savoy cabbage**
4 onions	**Pepper and salt**
2 rashers of bacon	**Sprinkling of chopped parsley and thyme**
2 carrots	**Stock made from 'trimmings'**
2oz diced bacon	

Truss the birds, place an onion inside each one and a rasher of bacon over each. Put them in a casserole with sliced carrots and onions cut into rings, the diced bacon, pepper and salt, parsley and thyme. Parboil the cabbage, drain it and cut into four. Pack this round the birds in the casserole, cover with the stock and simmer gently for 3 hours. Serve in the casserole with boiled potatoes.

The vineyard's partridge

An up-to-date version of an ancient recipe when vine leaves were used a great deal in cooking. Either use vine leaves from your greenhouse or conservatory or make a trip to your nearest vineyard. This is a real star for an East Anglian Food and Wine menu. Make sure that you serve the wine from the vineyard where you collected the leaves. Use young, early summer leaves before they toughen too much.

Ingredients for 4

2 partridges
4 vine leaves
4 slices oak smoked streaky bacon
2oz/60g butter
1 large glass of East Anglian grape juice
1 tablespoon sultanas
1 small measure brandy
A bunch of herbs
4 shallots
Salt and pepper to taste

Soak the sultanas in brandy for a few hours. Season the inside of the birds with salt and pepper. Blanch the vine leaves and pat them dry. Wrap the vine leaves around the birds, then the slices of streaky bacon. Secure with string.

Using a heavy, flameproof casserole dish, saute the partridges in butter for a few minutes on all sides. Add the grape juice, bouquet garni, shallots and seasoning. Cook, covered over low heat for 1 hour or until the meat feels tender under a knife. Add the soaked sultanas and finish cooking, uncovered, for a further 15 minutes. Remove string, halve the partridges and serve with the pan juices and trimmings.

Roast partridges on a nest

Ingredients for 4

A brace of birds
4 slices oak smoked bacon
4oz/120g sausage meat
1 thick slice East Anglian cured ham
1 egg
2 onions
2oz/60g butter
1 teaspoon chopped parsley
½ teaspoon thyme
1 glass East Anglian dry wine
Salt and pepper to taste

For the nest
1 bunch of watercress
4 large flat mushrooms
4 large squares of bread
Butter

Preheat the oven to 400°F, 200°C, gas mark 6.

Prepare the stuffing by mixing together the sausage meat, ham, cubed, the chopped partridge liver, egg, herbs and pepper. Spoon the stuffing inside the birds, then place a peeled onion inside each one. Lay the birds, breast down, in a roasting dish and roast for 30 minutes. Reduce the oven heat to 350°F, 180°C, gas mark 4. Turn the birds breast up, place the bacon on top and continue cooking for a further 15 minutes or until tender. Baste well on the way through.

A few minutes before serving, cut the bread in 4 squares. Skim some of the fat from the roasting pan, and quickly fry the bread until crisp and golden on both sides. Fry the mushrooms, whole, in the butter. Take the partridges out of the oven, cut them in half and serve each half on a 'nest' of nicely arranged bread, mushrooms and watercress. Make the gravy by adding the wine to the cooking juices. Thicken slightly by reducing over high heat. Serve in a gravy boat.

Pheasant with apples

Excellent with the East Anglian late apple 'D'Arcy Spice'.

Ingredients

1 pheasant
2lbs/1 kg apples
2oz/60g butter
1 onion
4 juniper berries
Pinch of thyme
1 bayleaf
1 glass East Anglian apple juice
Salt and pepper to taste

Peel and core the apples, but leave them whole. Saute the pheasant in a flameproof casserole dish until golden brown on all sides. Add onion, seasoning, herbs and apple juice. Surround with apples and simmer until tender. Serve with pan juices.

Lincolnshire pheasant with chicory

Once a unique Belgium vegetable, chicory is now grown very successfully in East Anglia, particularly in Lincolnshire. It is a very good winter salad vegetable, and its flavour, when cooked, blends very well with the gamey taste of pheasant.

Ingredients for 4

1 pheasant	**1lb/500g chicory**
2 slices oak smoked streaky bacon	**1 lemon**
2 carrots	**3oz/90g butter**
1 large onion	**1 small measure port**
A bunch of herbs	**Salt and pepper to taste**

Wrap the bacon around the pheasant. Secure with string. In a heavy, flameproof casserole dish, saute the pheasant in the melted butter until golden brown on all sides. Add the carrot, cut in chunks and the onion, quartered. Add bunch of herbs and seasoning, cover tightly and simmer for 1 hour or until tender turning the pheasant twice while cooking.

In the meantime clean and trim the chicory. Leave the pieces whole and place them in a saucepan with the remaining butter, the port, a small glass of water, a little lemon juice. Cover the pan and simmer the chicory over low heat for 30 minutes. Lift the pheasant from the casserole. Pour the pieces of chicory and their cooking stock in the casserole with the meat juices. Mix well, bring up to the boil and reduce the sauce.

Check seasoning. Serve the pheasant carved on a serving dish surrounded with the pieces of chicory. Serve the sauce separately in a gravy boat. It is not necessary to prepare another green vegetable. A few hash brown potatoes or a dish of oven scollop potatoes are ideal with this.

Roast pheasant with black pudding

The butchers and pork butchers of East Anglia are the masters of scrumptious sausages and excellent herby black pudding. The flavour of black pudding is delicious when mixed with other meats. Serve this dish with cooking apples, sliced and fried in butter as a vegetable. The three tastes combined are extremely good.

Ingredients for 4

1 pheasant
8oz/250g black pudding
1 onion
4 slices bread
3oz/90g butter
1 bunch watercress
Salt and pepper to taste

Preheat the oven to 425F, 200C, gas mark 7

Remove the black pudding skin and place, whole, inside the pheasant with plenty of freshly ground black pepper and the onion. Lay the bird, breast down, in a roasting pan, top with butter, salt and pepper and roast at the rate of 20 minutes per pound. To serve, spoon the black pudding from the pheasant. Carve the bird and keep it warm on a serving dish.

Fry the 4 slices of bread in a little fat gathered from the roasting pan. When crisp and brown on both sides, spread the black pudding over the bread. Sprinkle with freshly ground black pepper and serve around the meat with a garnish of watercress. Make a little gravy with the pan juices. Serve separately.

Roast pheasant with red cabbage

Ingredients for 4

1 pheasant
4oz/120g bacon pieces
1 onion, sliced
1 small red cabbage, shredded
1 glass of East Anglian white wine
2oz/60g butter
1oz/30g pork dripping or good lard
4 juniper berries
Black pepper to taste

Preheat the oven to 425F, 220C, gas mark 7.

Season the pheasant with salt and pepper, place a knob of butter on the breast and roast at 20 minutes per pound or until tender. Twenty minutes before serving, melt the lard in a heavy saucepan and saute the bacon pieces in it. Add the shredded red cabbage, the sliced onion, the juniper berries and a little black pepper. Cover and simmer gently.

Carve the pheasant. Make gravy by adding the wine to the pan juices. With a slotted spoon, transfer the cabbage to a shallow serving dish. Place the pieces of meat over it. Pass the gravy separately.

Potted rabbit

This will keep well in the refrigerator. It can be served with salad and crusty bread, or on toast. A fine main course or a delicious snack with a chilled glass of wine.

Ingredients

1 large rabbit
8oz/250g fat belly of pork, rindless
4oz/120g oak smoked streaky bacon
2 onions
2 carrots
1 clove of garlic (optional)
A large pinch of thyme
2 bayleaves
A few sprigs of parsley
A pinch of allspice
½ bottle East Anglian white wine
Salt and pepper to taste

Joint the rabbit and simmer gently over low heat with the white wine, onions, vegetables, herbs and seasoning. Add a glass of water if necessary. Cook for roughly 2 hours or until the meat falls off the bones. Remove bones, vegetables and herbs from the pot. Reserve rabbit meat.

Cut the belly of pork in thin strips, add them to the rabbit stock and simmer until very tender. Return the rabbit meat to the pan, make sure all stock has been absorbed. Shred the two meats with a fork. Check seasoning. Leave to cool. When cooled, press into jars, seal well and keep in a cool place for a few days.

Debenham potted rabbit

This is an ideal dish for a summer picnic. Mr Neave, butcher in Debenham, Suffolk, makes the traditional Suffolk sweet-cured black bacon; the flavour goes beautifully with the cold rabbit.

Ingredients for 4 to 6

1 large rabbit
12 slices sweet cured bacon
1 glass East Anglian white wine
Thyme, chopped parsley and ground bayleaf
Pepper to taste

Joint the rabbit. Pack it in an overproof dish in layers with the slices of bacon, herbs and black pepper. Pour the wine over the top of the meat and cook in a preheated oven (375F, 190C, gas mark 5) for two hours. When well cooked, remove the bones but leave meat in large pieces. Return to the cooking vessel and leave to cool in the stock, with the bacon for at least 24 hours before eating. Serve chilled, in slices, with a green salad.

Hollow meat casserole with apples

(A recipe from R.T. Harvey, game retailers in Norwich)

Ingredients

1 rabbit, jointed
2 large onions
½ pt/¼ litre of stock
8oz/250g streaky bacon
3oz/90g butter
1 garlic clove, crushed
bouquet garni
2 tablespoons flour
¼ pt/⅛ litre of white wine
1 Bramley apple, cored and peeled.

Dry rabbit well and roll in seasoned flour, then wrap each piece with slices of bacon. Secure with a wooden skewer and brown with sliced onions in butter. Alternatively brown rabbit pieces in the butter with coarsely diced bacon and onions. Place in casserole with wine and stock, garlic and bouquet garni, as well as the apple cut in large pieces. Cover and simmer until tender, about 1½ hours. When the rabbit is tender, remove bouquet garni and strain off the sauce. Reduce if necessary or thicken with flour mixed with a little stock. Pour back over rabbit and serve sprinkled with finely chopped parsley.

Supreme of rabbit with sorrel

Sorrel is a tart tasting herb. It has been used in this country since the Elizabethans and can be purchased at nurseries or herb garden specialists.

Ingredients for 4

1 rabbit, jointed	**1 pt/½ litre chicken stock**
½lb/250g sorrel	**2 egg yolks**
2oz/60g butter	**1 small pot of cream**
½oz/15g flour	**Salt and pepper**

Using a large, heavy flameproof dish, saute the rabbit pieces in the butter. Sprinkle with flour, mix well and cover gradually with the stock. Bring to the boil, lower the heat and simmer for 45 minutes to 1 hour according to size and tenderness of the rabbit. Wash the sorrel, remove the stems and cut the leaves in fine strips. Add to casserole, simmer for a further 15 minutes.

Transfer the meat to a serving dish and keep warm while you make the sauce. To make sauce: Beat the egg yolks with the cream in a small mixing bowl. Add one serving spoon of stock, mix well, add a little more stock. Return this mixture to the casserole with the remaining stock. Stirring constantly, leave the sauce to thicken over low heat. Check the seasoning and pour over the rabbit pieces. Serve with new potatoes.

Mustard rabbit

Tender, marinated rabbit roasted in a coating of the mustard of your choice.

Ingredients for 4

1 rabbit, whole	**A pinch of sage and a pinch of rosemary**
3 tablespoons oil	**Plenty of mustard**
salt and pepper	**1 teaspoon of double cream**
Thyme and ground bayleaf	**2 oz/60g butter**
1 clove	**A glass of East Anglian white wine**
1 carrot, sliced	

Marinate the rabbit for 24 hours in oil, pepper, salt, herbs, sliced onions and carrots

Preheat the oven to 400F, 200C, gas mark 6

Pat the rabbit dry and cover on all sides with mustard. Place in a roasting dish, and dot with butter. Add the peeled onions. Roast, basting frequently until very tender. Joint the rabbit and transfer to a warm serving dish. Make the mustard sauce by adding the white wine and then the teaspoon of double cream to the pan juices. Reduce slightly and pour over meat.

Coddenham jugged hare

An old recipe, given to me at the local pub, when I lived in Suffolk. A wholesome winter dish!

Place together in a large earthenware casserole, a jointed hare, 2lbs/1kg of chuck steak, 2 onions (one studded with cloves), 1 lb/500g carrots, a bunch of herbs. Cover with port, season with salt and pepper. Tightly seal with casserole lid, cook for 4 hours in a slow oven. Just before serving, add butter rolled in flour to thicken the sauce and adjust seasoning. Serve with winter vegetables and mashed potatoes.

The grape-pickers celebration hot pot

Ingredients for 8

1 hare, jointed
8oz/250g sliced lean belly pork
3oz/90g butcher's lard
1 dessertspoon flour
8oz/250g small pickling onions
6oz/180g firm green grapes
1oz/30g blanched almonds
2 tablespoons thick cream
A little freshly grated ginger
A little basil
A little thyme
Salt and pepper
A whole bottle of East Anglian white wine

Cube the belly of pork and saute in lard until golden brown in a large, heavy, flameproof dish. Set pork pieces aside and proceed likewise with jointed hare. When all the pieces have taken colour, sprinkle with the flour. Mix well. Pour ½ bottle of wine over the meat, bring quickly to the boil and boil for 5 minutes, add seasoning and herbs. Return pork pieces to the casseole with the peeled onions. Lower the heat, cover and cook over gentle heat for 1 hour. Add the remaining wine, boil once more and cook, covered, for a further hour or until tender (the cooking time depends on the quality and age of game).

Ten minutes before serving add the grapes and almonds. Finish cooking with pan uncovered. Add cream, mix well. Serve on a deep serving dish with large croutons of fried bread. Drink the same wine as used for the sauce.

Autumn orchard wild duck

Ingredients for 4

2 wild ducks
2oz/60g butter
1 onion, chopped
2 sticks celery, chopped
1 cooking apple, peeled and chopped
3oz/90g chopped hazelnuts
1 egg, beaten
2 thick slices brown bread
½ teaspoon grated orange rind
½ teaspoon grated lemon rind
½ teaspoon chopped parsley
¼ teaspoon rosemary
A pinch of mace
A little dry white wine
Salt and pepper

Preheat the oven to 425F, 230C, gas mark 8

Brown the chopped hazelnuts under the grill. Make breadcrumbs with the 2 slices of bread. Saute onions, celery and apple in a little butter until transparent. In a mixing bowl, combine hazelnuts, onion, celery and apple with grated rinds of citrus fruit. Stir in the breadcrumbs, herbs, beaten egg and just enough wine to make the mixture moist. Add salt and pepper, mix once more and spoon into ducks.

Lay the birds, breast down, on a rack in a roasting dish, roast for 30 minutes. Reduce heat to 375F, 190C, gas mark 5, roast for a further 1½ hours or until ducks no longer drip pink when pierced in thigh.

Venison chops with fresh cherry sauce

Ingredients for 4

4 or 8 chops according to size
2oz/60g butter
1 dessertspoon oil
Crushed peppercorns
Salt
Watercress for garnish

For the sauce
8oz/250g cherries – slightly unripe
1 small measure of port
A little mace
The juice of one orange
1 teaspoon finely grated orange rind
1 teaspoon redcurrant jelly
1 knob of butter the size of a walnut
A little arrowroot if required

Press peppercorns on both sides of chops and leave to stand for 1 hour. Prepare the cherry sauce: Place the orange juice, rind, port and mace in a pan. Bring to the boil. Lower the heat, add the stoned cherries, simmer over very gentle heat until cherries are tender. Add butter, arrowroot and redcurrant jelly just before serving.

To cook the chops: Saute the peppered chops in butter and oil in a frying pan, sealing the meat on both sides. Lower the heat and cook for the desired time just as you would a steak. Salt towards end of cooking. Serve on individual plates, garnished with watercress. Pass the cherry sauce separately in a gravy boat.

Marinated roast haunch of venison
(with mustard sauce)

Ingredients for 6

1 small haunch of venison
2oz/60g butter
6 shallots
1 tablespoon coarse mustard
½ teaspoon honey

For the marinade
2 onions, sliced
2 carrots, sliced
3 tablespoons oil
¼ bottle East Anglian white wine
1 stick celery, chopped
2 garlic cloves, crushed
Thyme and crushed bayleaf
A few peppercorns
A little rosemary
2 cloves

In a saucepan, place the wine, celery, garlic, peppercorns and herbs. Add the sliced onions and carrots, bring to the boil and simmer for 30 minutes. Leave to cool totally. Pour over the venison and leave to marinate, covered, for 48 hours in a cool place, turning the meat morning and evening.

To cook the meat: Preheat the oven to 425F, 220C, gas mark 7. Pat the meat dry. Peel the shallots. Place the meat in a roasting dish surrounded by the shallots. Dot the butter on top and roast for 20 minutes per pound. Strain the marinade through a nylon sieve. Remove all vegetables. Reduce the marinade liquid to half its amount by boiling over high heat. Set aside for the sauce. When the meat is cooked, transfer to meat dish and carve.

Make the sauce: Add reduced marinade, mustard, honey, salt and pepper to the meat juices. Thicken if necessary with a little butter rolled in flour. Serve in a gravy boat.

NB. A small amount of sour cream may be added to the sauce.

Rabbit Royale

To conclude this chapter a very special recipe . . . from the kitchens of Sandringham. This recipe was kindly given to me by Diana Dickerson of Swaffham

Ingredients

1 rabbit	**1 shallot, chopped**
Salt and pepper	**2oz/60g suet**
1 teaspoon of grated lemon rind	**1 egg**
2oz/60g breadcrumbs	**1 rasher of bacon**
1 teaspoon chopped parsley	**Fat for basting**

Wash rabbit and season well. Skin and chop tomatoes finely, mix with lemon rind, breadcrumbs, parsley, thyme, chopped shallot and suet. Add beaten egg and stuff rabbit with this mixture. Truss it and lay bacon over back. Roast for 50 to 60 minutes in hot oven (375 to 400F, gas 5 to 6). Baste. Remove bacon 10 minutes before serving. Serve rabbit garnished with grilled bacon rolls and freshly made tomato sauce.

Tomato sauce

Ingredients

1oz/30g bacon
1 onion
1 small carrot
½oz/15g butter
4 medium size tomatoes (fresh, bottled or canned)
½ dessertspoon rice flour
liquid from canned or bottled tomato
Salt and pepper
Lemon juice, sugar
Grated nutmeg

Slice onion and carrot. Place in saucepan with bacon and fry in fat without browning for 10 minutes. Slice and add tomatoes, cook for 5 minutes. Sprinkle in rice flour, add tomato juice, stir until the mixture boils, reduce heat and simmer for 45 minutes. Season and add lemon juice, sugar and nutmeg to taste.

Poultry

Poultry

Poultry provides a vital part of the nation's diet and since the early 18th century, when East Anglian turkeys and geese were made to walk from Norwich to London, Norfolk has been the undisputed centre for the production of Britain's Christmas meal. Old established firms like Button of Diss, Norfolk have behind them the accumulated experience of 65 years in the poultry business and are now the largest producers of geese and ducklings in the U.K.

Norfolk ducklings are on the menu in top hotels and restaurants all over the country and often the prime choice of the housewife for a special dinner party. Despite the fact that some turkey breeders encouraged by public demand sadly decided to cut corners and provide quantity rather than quality, most farmers, like Derek Kelly, of Kelly Turkeys near Chelmsford, have stuck to their guns and in recent years have provided first quality fresh turkeys and revived the sale of old and tasty breeds like the Bronze or the Norfolk Black. Free-range chicken and cockerel breeders are to be found throughout the region and in Diss and immediate surrounding Norfolk and Suffolk farms, Mr Cairns of Ark Foods breeds free-range guinea-fowls fed on wheat and corn. There was a time when guinea-fowl was game but because of recent EEC rules it is now in the poultry category.

From the huge array of poultry products in East Anglia, I have chosen some old favourites and some of my own creations, for you . . .

A REPAST OF CHICKEN

I was listening, recently to a New York radio interview with Anthony Matthews, President of Food From From Britain, in the U.S.A. He was stressing the point that the quality of the products is so good that to enjoy British food at its best, the answer is to keep it simple. I could not agree more. And to make a meal memorable it is often unnecessary to hit the taste buds with too many mixed flavours. Here are the recipes for a meal which I served, one Sunday, to friends in Norfolk. One large farm cockerel provided us with three different courses. Followed by an open fruit tart it gave the whole meal a kind of ancient traditional splendour, back to the days when the home-fattened fowl was the treat for special occasions.

With vegetables, asparagus and spinach from the garden the meal comprised:

Chicken and Vegetable Clear Soup

Mousse of Chicken Breast with Asparagus

Cutlets of Dark Meat with Spinach

Chicken and vegetable clear soup

Ingredients for 4

1 large farm cockerel
4 young carrots, sliced
2 sticks celery, sliced
4oz/120g button mushrooms, sliced
2 onions, one studded with 2 cloves
Fresh thyme, bayleaf, coriander, lovage – tied
2 pts/1 litre water
1 glass East Anglian dry white wine
Salt and pepper

Place all the ingredients except the mushrooms in a large stewpan. Bring to the boil, skim once or twice and then, reducing heat, simmer until the cockerel is just cooked. Leave to cool in the pan. Then lift the poultry from the pan – the meat is used for the two following courses. To prepare the clear soup, remove onions, slide the mushrooms and boil them in the stock for 5 minutes. Adjust seasoning and serve.

Cold chicken mousse with asparagus

Ingredients for the mousse:

The whole breast of cockerel
¼pt/⅛ litre double cream, whipped
2 teaspoons gelatine
2 large tablespoons chicken stock
2 dessertspoons of green peppercorns

Place white meat in food blender, reduce to a puree, add green peppercorns and adjust salt seasoning. In a pan, soften gelatine in the chicken stock, add to the chicken puree and mix well. Leave to cool slightly then fold in the whipped cream. Divide the mixture between 4 buttered ramequin dishes. Keep in refrigerator until last minute.

Ingredients for the asparagus garnish

16 asparagus
1 small pot of single cream
2 tablespoons chicken stock
Chopped chervil and chives
A squeeze of lemon juice

Boil or steam the asparagus, making sure they stay quite firm. Drain well and chill. To serve, mix together cream, chicken stock, herbs and lemon juice. Spoon this cold sauce on to individual serving plates. Turn a chicken mousse on to each one and lay 4 asparagus per plate near the mousse.

Cutlets of dark meat with spinach

Ingredients

The cockerel thighs and drumsticks
1 egg, beaten
Breadcrumbs
1 lemon
1lb/500g cooked leaf spinach
Butter
Salt and pepper

Remove meat from bones in large chunks. Press together and immediately dip in beaten egg and breadcrumbs. Melt some butter in a frying pan and as soon as it bubbles, fry the chicken cutlets in it. In the meantime, season spinach with melted butter, salt and pepper. Serve chicken cutlets on a bed of spinach, with a little of the cooking butter and a slice of lemon.

Bryan Pickering's chicken thigh with tarragon

Ingredients for 4

4 large or 8 small chicken thighs	**Salt and pepper**
1 oz/30g chopped tarragon leaves	**Butter**

Remove bone from chicken thigh and sprinkle tarragon in cavity. Secure with cocktail stick and roast with butter, salt and pepper.

Peartree chicken breast supreme

(a recipe compiled after a visit to Peartree Poultry farm Essex)

Ingredients for 4

8 small chicken breast fillets	**1oz/30g butter**
8oz/250g lean sausage meat	**1pt/½ litre chicken stock**
1oz/30g ground hazelnuts	**1 small pot double cream**
1 egg	**Salt and pepper**
A few chopped tarragon leaves	

Mix sausage meat with hazelnuts, tarragon leaves, salt and pepper. Bind mixture with the beaten egg. Divide mixture in 4 portions and spread in between 2 chicken breast fillets. Secure with string to hold stuffing. Bring stock to the boil and then, reducing heat, poach the chicken fillets for 30 to 40 minutes according to thickness. Lift off stock and keep warm. Bring the stock to the boil and reduce by half, add cream, butter and adjust seasoning. Cut string off chicken breasts and serve with the sauce and creamed or sauteed potatoes and broccoli or spinach.

Summer savoury tartlets

Peas, chicken breast and mushrooms in a fine pastry case. Ideal for a light luncheon with a chilled East Anglian wine.

Ingredients for 4

4 individual shortpastry cases baked blind
2 large chicken breasts
½lb/120g button mushrooms
1 thick slice of sweet cure ham
1 chicken stock cube
1 onion
1 glass East Anglian white wine
1 egg yolk
1 knob butter, size of walnut
Double cream

Poach the chicken breast with the onion in chicken stock and wine. When nearly cooked, add peas and cook for a further 8 minutes, then add the button mushrooms, sliced. Simmer for a further 5 minutes. Cut ham in small strips, and make the sauce. In a small mixing bowl put cream and egg yolk, mix well and add a tablespoon of chicken stock, then a little more until you have reached the quantity of sauce required. Transfer into pan and whisk in the butter over very low heat. The sauce should be just thick enough to coat the back of a spoon. Dice the chicken breasts. Mix together with ham and vegetables. Add sauce and pile inside the pastry cases. Reheat in warm oven for 10 minutes.

Chicken Fricassee

Ingredients for 4

4 breasts or chicken thighs
2 shallots
4 tomatoes
¼lb/120g bacon pieces
1 mugful chicken stock
1 glass East Anglian white wine
Parsley, thyme and bayleaf
Salt and pepper
2oz/60g butter
1 dessertspoon oil

Using a heavy, flameproof casserole dish, fry peeled shallots and bacon in the butter/oil mixture. Remove from pan and now brown the chicken pieces on all sides. Add the peeled tomatoes, stir well. Return shallots and bacon to the dish, add chicken stock, wine, herbs and seasoning. Cover and simmer for 1 hour. Serve from dish with potatoes and a green vegetable.

Novoli farm roast chicken

When I visited Mr Manning at his free-range poultry farm in Purleigh, Essex, we came to the conclusion that in the case of a prime quality bird it is a great shame to alter the flavour with highly seasoned stuffing. 'I like to taste the chicken, when we roast one, and if my wife decides to prepare a stuffing she usually cooks it separately' said Mr Manning. Here is a very simple recipe which will in no way impair the true flavour of a farm free-range chicken but just add a little smoothness to the gravy.

Place a dessertspoon of fresh cream cheese with salt and pepper inside the chicken. Season the outer skin with salt and pepper. Dot butter over breast and thighs and roast in warm oven for 25 minutes per pound, basting well. To make the gravy, spoon the cream cheese out and mix with the pan juices and a dessertspoon of dry East Anglian white wine. Adjust seasoning. Serve in a gravy boat with the roast meat.

Potted duck

Ingredients

2 farm ducks
6oz/180g butcher's lard
½ teaspoon ground bayleaf
½ teaspoon mace
1 sprig fresh thyme
1 sprig rosemary
4 sage leaves
Salt and freshly ground black pepper
1 glass East Anglian dry white wine

You will need a deep large casserole dish or even better a large glazed earthenware pot. Remove duck's parson's nose and the gland which is immediately above it – it gives duck a very unpleasant taste.

With a fork blend lard with salt and pepper, mace and bayleaf. Rub well over the ducks. Put them in the deep dish as close together as possible, placing a tied bunch of thyme, rosemary and sage between them. Add wine. Seal tight with the lid. Bake in a low oven for 4 hours. When done, remove bunch of herbs and bones. Adjust seasoning. Pack meat in potting jars adding a little fat as you go along. Cover with melted fat. Leave to cool. When cold, seal and keep in a cold room for at least 2 days before eating. It will keep for weeks in the refrigerator.

Eat cold with crusty bread or hot toast spread with a little of the deliciously flavoured dripping. Serve with a green salad made of lettuce, dandelions or spinach tossed with oil and vinegar dressing, chopped chervil, chives and a few walnut kernels.

Potted duck and pea pie

A very flavoursome pie to be eaten hot or cold. The pastry is deliciously shortened with the fat from the potted meat. A good stand-by recipe when entertaining guests around Christmas time.

Ingredients for the pastry
8oz/250g flour
4oz/120g potted duck fat
Water

Proceed as usual. Roll in a ball, chill for 1 hour, then roll to required thickness.

Ingredients for pie filling
1 large serving spoon of potted duck per person
8oz/250g garden peas, shelled
2 shallots, chopped
1 small glass East Anglian dry white wine
1 dessertspoon flour
1 glass water

Preheat oven to 425F, 220C, gas mark 7

Boil peas in salted water until tender, drain well. Remove fat from around duck meat. Peel and chop shallots. In a frying pan, place 1 dessertspoon of duck fat. As soon as it starts bubbling, add chopped shallots, let them take colour, sprinkle the flour over them and mix well. Add wine and water and, stirring, cook for 5 minutes. Leave to cool. Blend together duck meat, peas and gravy. Spoon into a pie dish. Cover with pastry. Make hole in the centre and bake in the preheated oven for 30 minutes or until pastry is golden brown and centre piping hot.

Pot roasted duck with onions

Ingredients for 4

1 large duck,
2½oz/75g belly of pork
The duck liver
20 pickling onions
1 garlic clove, crushed
2 tablespoons fresh breadcrumbs
1 mugful chicken stock
2 sprigs of thyme
12 sage leaves
Salt and pepper
1 glass East Anglian white wine

Preheat oven to its maximum. Remove the gland situated over parson's nose.

Place duck on a rack over a roasting pan and roast for 30 minutes on maximum heat, pricking the skin with a fork. Most of the surplus fat should melt away. Mix together breadcrumbs, crushed garlic, salt and pepper with the chopped duck liver, 5 sage leaves, chopped and a few thyme leaves. Place inside duck.

Peel the onions. Remove rind from belly of pork and cut in strips. Using a deep, flameproof casserole dish, fry onions and belly of pork in 2 tablespoons of duck fat scooped from the roasting pan. When golden brown add the duck, the remaining herbs and warmed-up chicken stock with white wine. Cover and simmer over gentle heat for 2 hours or until duck is totally cooked. Transfer and carve duck on to a meat plate, garnished with onions and pork pieces.

Remove excess fat from the sauce. Bring to the boil to shorten slightly. Serve with meat and boiled vegetables of your choice.

Roast duckling with fresh blackcurrants and portwine sauce

Ingredients for 4

1 farm duck
½pt/¼ litre stock made from giblets
½ juice of lemon
2 tablespoons of blackcurrants, underripe
1 large measure of port
1 onion, peeled
Salt and pepper

Preheat the oven to 350F, 180C, gas mark 4

Remove gland from parson's nose. Remove giblets and use for stock with water, seasoning thyme, bayleaf and one sage leaf. Prick duck skin all over with a fork. Season with salt and pepper and roast on a rack in a roasting pan at the rate of 35 minutes per pound. When cooked, remove duck to a serving dish and keep warm while making the sauce.

For the sauce: Tip excess cooking fat from roasting pan. Add stock to cooking juices together with blackcurrants, port and lemon juice. Bring to the boil and reduce to thicken. Add a little arrowroot if required. Carve duck, using a slotted spoon, decorate duck pieces with blackcurrants. Serve gravy separately in a gravyboat, having adjusted seasoning. Serve with new potatoes, peas or green beans.

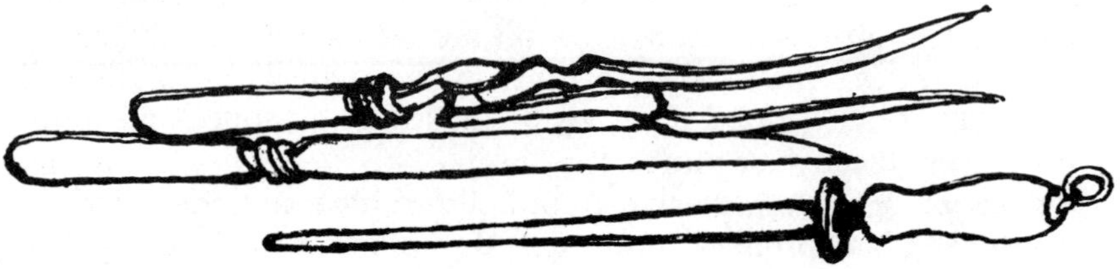

Mushroom stuffed duckling breast
(with the compliments of A.E. Button & Sons, Diss, Norfolk)

A marjoram-flavoured breadcrumb filling, dotted with mushrooms and enriched with ground almonds. Accompany with cranberry sauce, gravy, creamed potatoes and vegetables to taste.

Ingredients for 2

1 duckling breast joint
2oz/60g brown breadcrumbs
1 shallot, peeled and finely chopped
4oz/120g mushrooms
1 teaspoon marjoram
1oz/30g ground almonds
1 to 2 teaspoons cold milk
Salt and pepper

Preheat oven to 350F, 180C, gas mark 4

Remove surplus fat from breast joint. Make the stuffing by mixing breadcrumbs with chopped mushrooms, salt and pepper, marjoram and almonds, bind together with milk. Pack into breast cavity and secure with string to hold stuffing in place. Stand duck breast on a rack in a roasting pan, skin side uppermost. Prick all over with fork and season with salt and pepper. Roast for 1 hour 10 minutes. Then increase oven heat to 425F, 220C, gas mark 7 and continue roasting for a further 15 minutes to crispen the skin. To serve, cut into 2 portions, lengthwise.

ROAST GUINEA FOWL

The meat of guinea fowl is succulent and has a taste all of its own. Roast it with butter and seasoning, basting frequently and serve it with gravy made from the pan juices and a few sprigs of watercress, to discover its true flavour. On the other hand, here are two recipes which not only capture the flavour of the bird but create an altogether splendid flavour. I recommend the first one for a special dinner party.

Suffolk guinea fowl with apples

Ingredients for 4

1 guinea fowl
4 unripe dessert apples
½lb/250g Suffolk sweet-cured black bacon
2oz/60g butter
1 dessertspoon double cream
1 small measure brandy
Salt and pepper to taste

Preheat the oven to 425F, 220C, gas mark 7

Peel and core the apples. Cut bacon slices in small strips. Melt the butter in a frying pan and saute the bacon in it without letting it take too much colour. Remove bacon from butter with a slotted spoon. Pour butter over the guinea fowl laid breast down in a roasting dish. Spoon the bacon pieces inside the apples. Place around the bird. Roast for 20 minutes per pound, basting fowl and apples two or three times while cooking. Remove apples from pan as soon as they are cooked, keep warm in foil.

To serve: Transfer the guinea fowl to a warm serving dish, carve it in quarters and surround it with the stuffed apples. Add cream, brandy and maybe a little water to the pan juices, scrape well around the dish with a wooden spatula. Bring to the boil and pour immediately over the meat.

Braised guinea fowl with mushrooms and celery

Ingredients for 4

1 guinea fowl
1 large head of celery
2 shallots, peeled
½lb/250g flat mushrooms
2oz/60g butter
Water
Salt and pepper to taste

Preheat the oven to 425F, 220C, gas mark 7

Place guineafowl in a deep roasting pan. Surround it with chopped celery and mushrooms as well as the two shallots. Season with salt and pepper. Pour one small glass of water over the vegetables. Dot with butter and braise uncovered in oven for 1 hour. Serve straight from the dish with boiled potatoes.

GOOSE

'To eat a goose on Michaelmas Day might be a tradition all over England, but in Norfolk it is law' said John Adlard from his farm in Pulham Market, near Diss Norfolk. The chairman of the British Goose Producer's Association went on to explain the origins of the tradition. Is it because Queen Elizabeth I happened to be eating goose on that day when Sir Francis Drake gave her the good news of English victory over the Spanish Armada? Or is it to follow a long country tradition when geese, fattened on the harvest gleanings were used by tenants to pay rent to the Lord of the Manor? Whichever reason, there is something very particular about Michaelmas Day in Norfolk: everywhere else in the country the Feast of St. Michael is celebrated on September 29th but in Norfolk, for reasons no-one is able to discover, it is celebrated on October 11th.

However, here are a few recipes which will fit the occasion:

First a few rules on how to roast a goose (*with the compliments of the British Goose Producers' Association*).

How to roast a goose:

Preliminaries:

1) After cleaning, remove the wishbone. This enables the breast to be carved more easily
2) Stuff and truss the bird. This keeps in the stuffing as well as holding in the legs.
3) Lightly pierce the skin with a needle to encourage the fat to run out.

Roasting:

Goose is best roasted at high initial temperature to draw off excess fat.

8/10lb bird – 45 minutes at 425F, 220C, gas mark 7 then 1¾ to 2 hours at 325F, 170C, gas 3

10/12lb bird – 45 minutes at 425F, 220C, gas mark 7 then 2 to 2½ hours at 325F, 170C, Gas 3

Start the roasting with the bird on one side for a third of the time. Turn on its other side for an equal time, and finally place it breast side up. Baste every 15/20 minutes but remove excess fat from roasting pan at intervals. Allow it to rest for twenty minutes in a warm place before carving.

N.B. Goose fat makes the best roast potatoes. Poured in a jar it will keep well in the refrigerator. Use for other recipes as page 90.

Michaelmas roast goose with herbs and celery

Ingredients

1 oven ready goose	**2 sprig of rosemary**
2 heads of celery with leaves	**1 glass East Anglian white wine**

Place rosemary and celery leaves inside the goose with salt and pepper. Roast as recommended above. Serve with roast potatoes and braised celery.

Michaelmas goose with potato stuffing and spiced pears

(with compliments of A.E. Button & Sons, Diss, Norfolk)

Ingredients

1 oven ready goose
Salt and pepper

For the stuffing
6 large potatoes, peeled, cooked and mashed
1 large onion, chopped
4 slices streaky bacon, chopped
1 teaspoon salt
Freshly ground black pepper
12oz/350g pork sausage meat
1 tablespoon chopped fresh parsley
1 teaspoon fresh thyme
1 teaspoon fresh sage, chopped

Combine all the ingredients for the stuffing, mix well then pack firmly into the body cavity of the goose. Close opening with a skewer. Roast as above. To test if the goose is cooked, pierce the thigh with a skewer: it will be ready when the juices run clear.

Spiced pears

12oz/350g granulated sugar
½pt/¼ litre white wine vinegar
½ cinnamon sticks
2 level teaspoons whole allspice
8 cloves
2lbs/1kg firm dessert pears

Measure sugar and vinegar into a saucepan, add cinnamon and other spices tied up in muslin. Stir over gentle heat to dissolve sugar and set aside. Peel, core and cut pears into eighths and add to saucepan. Bring to boil and simmer gently until pears are tender. Remove pears with slotted spoon and place in bowl. Discard spices. Return saucepan to heat, boil until syrup is quite thick, then pour over pears. It is preferable to prepare the pears at least the day before and keep covered in the refrigerator.

Serve goose with stuffing, a thin gravy made from the giblets and the spiced pears just warmed through.

Cold roast goose

Cold goose is excellent. Prepare it without stuffing, roast as mentioned above and leave to cool whole. Serve, carved with a salad of frisee endive, tossed in oil and vinegar dressing with little pieces of fried bread and fried smoked bacon. Serve at the same time Onion and Gooseberry relish (see recipe page 141), or Melanie Knibbs' Quince Jelly.

Quince jelly with lemon

For every 1lb/500g of quince allow ⅛pt of water. Put the fruit and water into a preserving pan and simmer over gentle heat for about ¾ hour or until very soft. Strain through a jelly bag. Add 1lb/500g sugar and half the juice of a lemon to every pint of liquid strained. Allow sugar to dissolve. Bring to the boil and boil hard until set – about 20 minutes. Pour into jars adding a few strips of the lemon peel to each jar.

Goose breast fillets with sorrel

Ingredients for 4

4 slices of breast fillets
1lb/500g sorrel
2oz/60g goose fat (see page 87)
½ teaspoon redcurrant jelly
2 tablespoons double cream

Remove skin and fat from the fillets. Melt the goose dripping in a frying pan, as soon as it bubbles saute the fillets on both sides until they take colour, lower the heat, season with salt and pepper and cook, covered, for 20 minutes. In the meantime remove stalks from sorrel. Blanch for 5 minutes in boiling water. Drain well.

When goose is cooked, remove from pan and keep warm. Place the cooked sorrel in the pan together with cream and redcurrant jelly. Adjust seasoning. Spoon on individual plates, place a goose fillet over the sorrel sauce and serve with sauteed potatoes.

TURKEY

Norfolk Christmas turkey

1 oven ready Bronze or Black Turkey
Salt and pepper
Butter

For the stuffing:
1lb/500g ground pork
¼lb/120g smoked streaky bacon
¼lb/120g fresh brown breadcrumbs
1 dessertspoon grated carrot
1 dessertspoon chopped mushroom
1 egg
1 teaspoon chopped parsley
½ teaspoon finely grated lemon rind
1 teaspoon thyme
1 teaspoon chopped lovage
Salt and pepper

Four hours before roasting the turkey prepare the stuffing: Cut the bacon in very fine strips and blend in with all other ingredients. Pack tight inside bird. Secure end with a skewer. With a fork work freshly ground sea salt and black pepper into a large piece of unsalted butter. Using the blade of a knife spread the seasoned butter on all sides of the turkey. Place the stuffed bird, breast down in a roasting pan and leave in a cool room until cooking starts.

Preheat the oven to 400F, 200C, gas mark 6. Place the bird in warm oven and cook for 25 minutes per pound including the weight of stuffing. Lower the heat to 350F, 180C, gas mark 4 after the first hour. Baste frequently, serve with roast potatoes, vegetables and gravy made with giblets cooked with half water, half East Anglian wine and a bunch of herbs.

East Anglian Thanksgiving turkey

(To all our American friends based in East Anglia)

Stuff turkey with sausage meat and herbs, roast as above and serve with streaky bacon rolls filled with a vegetarian pumpkin forcemeat.

For the forcemeat:

½ small pumpkin	**1oz/30g chopped nuts**
2 large potatoes	**Salt and pepper**
1 small onion, grated finely	**A little flour**
A touch of grated ginger	

Boil and mash the potatoes. Pare the pumpkin and cut it in thin slices. Place in a saucepan with butter, cover and simmer gently until cooked. Mash it. Blend together potatoes, cooked pumpkin, finely grated onion, ginger, nuts and seasoning. Roll in small balls in flour, encase with a small rasher of streaky bacon and cook around the turkey for 30 minutes.

Boiled turkey supreme

Young turkey, boiled with vegetables is very good. The oyster stuffing recipe given on page 27 goes very well with it.

Ingredients

One young Bronze or Black Norfolk turkey	**2 egg yolks**
Oyster stuffing	**1 glass East Anglian dry white wine**
1 carrot	**1 small pot double cream**
1 large onion, studded with 1 clove	**1 teaspoon cornflour**
1 stick of celery	**Salt and pepper to taste**

Stuff and truss the turkey. Place it in a large stewpan with vegetables, water and a glass of wine. Add seasoning, bring to the boil, skim once or twice and, reducing the heat, simmer for 2 hours. Lift the bird from the pan. Carve and transfer to a serving dish while you make the sauce.

For the sauce. Place egg yolks and cream with a little seasoning in a bowl. Add the cornflour and mix well. Slowly add some stock until you get the quantity of sauce you will require. Transfer to a saucepan and over very low heat thicken the sauce, stirring all the time to avoid curdling. Serve slices of turkey with a spoonful of oyster stuffing, new potatoes and a green vegetable. Pass the white sauce separately.

Pork and pork products

Pork and pork products

The prime meat of the region, East Anglian pork is of excellent quality. Much leaner than it used to be by the requirements of a modern health-conscious society, it is the basis of splendid products to be found at local butchers throughout East Anglia and indeed the whole of Britain.

Good sausages abound, all proudly bearing their name of origin, such as the Old Epping sausage, the Royale Cambridge, the much prized Newmarket or the sagey Lincolnshire. Those are only a few of the well-known brands but it would seem that, wherever I went, I was recommended to try the prize winning local sausage – and I did. They were mostly excellent, leaving the factory-made bundles of fat, gluten, artificial flavouring and preservatives, looking very pale indeed.

There are other scrumptious things to be found, such as the Lincolnshire stuffed chine, pork pies and haslet, Huntingdonshire fidget pies, ham and bacon cured and smoked in different original ways throughout the region. Chitterlings are still to be found in Great Yarmouth and other towns in the region and, outside Norwich, I tasted the best black pudding I have ever had in this country.

With the addition of locally grown vegetables, herbs of all kind or even fruit like pears or apples to follow older traditions, East Anglian pork and its massive range of products can be eaten from breakfast to supper year round.

Suffolk apple stuffed pork tenderloin

I always thought apply juice much too sweet to use with meat, until I discovered the juice made by the Peake family, at Boxford, near Colchester. The brand name is Copella and it is just pure pressed apples without any additives, not even water. It is ideal for sauces as it is thicker than other juices and slightly tarter. Combined with the taste of Suffolk sweet-cured 'black bacon' it is very good.

Ingredients for 4

2 pork tenderloin
½lb/250g good sausage meat
2 glasses pure apple juice
4 slices Suffolk sweet-cured bacon
1oz/30g butter
2 sage leaves, chopped
1 cooking apple
1 small onion, chopped
A few chopped chives
Salt and pepper to taste

Preheat the oven to 400F, 200C, gas mark 6

Cut each tenderloin lengthwise, not quite through. Flatten out. Season with a little salt and pepper. Now prepare the stuffing: Heat ½ glass of apple juice with butter and sage. Stir into the onions, sausage meat, chives, the apple, chopped but not peeled and a little pepper. Spread stuffing over one flattened loin. Top with the second one, lay the bacon slices over the meat and secure with either string or skewers. Place the meat in a roasting dish. Warm remaining apple juice, pour over the meat and roast uncovered for 1 hour or until well done. Make gravy with the pan juices.

Leg of pork roasted with herbs and vegetables

Ingredients

One piece of leg of pork on the bone
2 onions
2 cloves
2 large carrots
1 good size leek
1 clove of garlic
Parsley, thyme and ground bayleaf
4oz/120g of smoked bacon pieces
4 tomatoes
A large knob of butter
1 glass of East Anglian white wine
Seasalt and pepper to taste

Preheat the oven to 425°F, 200°C, gas mark 7

Peel the garlic clove and insert it alongside the bone. Peel and wash the vegetables and cut them in large chunks. Insert the cloves into one onion. Place the meat in the centre of a roasting pan, surround it with the vegetables and bacon pieces mixed, sprinkle with herbs, freshly ground seasalt and pepper. Dot pieces of butter over the meat and place in oven for 20 minutes. Then, reduce the oven heat to 350F, 180C, gas mark 4 add the glass of white wine and, basting from time to time, continue cooking at the rate of 35 minutes per pound. Twenty minutes before serving, place the tomatoes whole, around the meat. Serve the meat sliced, with the pan juices, and the garnish of vegetables.

Suffolk porkburger parcels

The home-cured streaky bacon made by Peter Neave, in Debenham, Suffolk is really rather special and well worth a detour when in the area. I used it for the following recipe which makes an easy to prepare lunchtime snack served with baked potatoes and a tossed salad. Of course any good tendersweet cured bacon can be used.

Ingredients for 4

1lb/500g freshly ground lean pork
8 slices sweet-cured streaky bacon
4 sage leaves or fresh coriander
Pepper to taste
A little salt
4 squares of foil
A little oil

Preheat the oven at 425°F, 220°C, gas mark 7

Season the minced pork with salt and freshly ground pepper and divide in four portions. Make a ball with each portion then flatten it in a burger shape. Lay the sage or coriander over the meat and wrap the bacon around each burger. Place at the centre of lightly oiled foil. Wrap the foil tightly around the meat and bake in the preheated oven for 25 minutes.

Pork chops with onions and tomatoes

Ingredients for 4

4 lean pork chops
4 onions
6 tomatoes
Salt and pepper to taste
1 tablespoon of East Anglian White wine
2oz/60g of butter
A little oil

Using a flameproof casserole dish, saute the pork chops in the butter/oil mixture until brown on all sides. Add the onions, and saute with the meat. Now add the peeled tomatoes. Season well and simmer, covered, over low heat until the chops are tender. Transfer the chops to a serving dish. Add wine to the cooking juices, bring quickly to the boil, check seasoning. Pour the sauce over the chops.

Pork and celeriac casserole

Celeriac, this chunky tasty winter vegetable once cooked with meat gives a general smoky flavour to the dish. Lovage, which of itself has a slight celery taste, is the ideal herb for this recipe.

Ingredients for 4

2lbs/1kg cubed pork pieces
1 celeriac
8oz/250g button mushrooms
1 carrot, sliced
1 onion, quartered
1 lovage leaf, chopped
Salt and pepper to taste

Using a heavy flameproof casserole, saute the meat and onion in the butter until golden brown. Add the sliced carrot, lovage leaf and just enough warm water to cover the meat. Season and simmer, covered, for ¾ hour. Now, peel and cut the celeriac into chunks, slice the mushrooms. Add the two vegetables to the casserole, mixing well with the meat and continue simmering until the celeriac pieces are tender. Serve straight from the dish with the stock which can be slightly thickened with a little arrowroot.

Fens pork tenderloin

Thin slices of pork tenderloin, with a puree of leeks. A quick and easy meal to prepare

Ingredients for 4

1 large pork tenderloin
1lb/500g leeks
3oz/90g butter
1 tablespoon thick cream
A pinch of nutmeg
A little East Anglian white wine
Black pepper and salt to taste

Wash and chop the leeks. Place them in a deep frying pan with 2oz/60g butter. Cook gently without letting them take colour, over low heat, stirring from time to time. Puree, adding pepper, nutmeg, cream and salt to taste. Keep warm.

Divide the tenderloin in thin round slices, flatten them. Fry in the remaining butter for a few minutes on each side. This cut of meat is very tender, therefore the cooking time must be quick, otherwise the meat will toughen. When meat and the butter in which they cooked are a nice golden colour, transfer on individual plates, spoon some leek puree in the centre of each one. Serve with sauteed potatoes.

Hearty all East Anglian hot pot

A nourishing and deliciously tasty mixture of pork, bacon and duck cooked with all the East Anglian root vegetables, served with cabbage.

Ingredients for 6 or more

1 farm duck, cleaned and quartered
2lbs/1kg lean pork pieces
1 small smoked bacon knuckle
4 carrots
3 onions
1 parsnip
2 turnips
2 leeks
A large bunch of herbs (thyme, bay etc. . .)
1 garlic clove
1 head of celeriac
4 large flat mushrooms
½ bottle East Anglian wine
½pt/¼ litre chicken stock
Pepper and salt to taste
1 teaspoon tomato puree

Preheat the oven to 475F, 240C, gas mark 9

Place the duck pieces on a rack over a roasting pan and roast, in the hot oven, for 30 minutes. By then the duck should have shed most of its fat. Keep aside. Now spoon a small amount of duck fat in a large flameproof casserole and brown the pork pieces with the onions. Add the wine and bring to the boil. In any order, add the remaining ingredients i.e. duck pieces, vegetables, pork knuckle, herbs, chicken stock and tomato puree.

Bring to the boil once more, and having reduced the oven heat to 375F, 190C, gas mark 5, place in oven for 2 hours or until meats are tender. Before serving, degrease the surface of the dish with a large spoon, check seasoning and serve straight from the dish with cabbage and potatoes, plenty of crusty bread and a bottle or two of East Anglian wine.

Summer pork casserole

Ingredients for 4

2lbs/1kg lean pork pieces
6 good size spring onions
6 courgettes
¼lb/120g button mushrooms
1 garlic clove (optional)
1 sprig of tarragon
1 glass of water
½ glass East Anglian white wine
2oz/60g butter
1 tablespoon oil
Salt and pepper to taste

Saute the pork pieces and chopped onions in a flameproof casserole with the butter/oil mixture. Only saute a small amount at a time, so that the meat colours well on all sides. Add the sliced unpeeled courgettes, herbs and sliced mushrooms, stir well and add the wine. Cover and simmer over gentle heat for 2 hours. The vegetables form a puree around the meat. The sauce should be very short. Check seasoning. Serve with young carrots and potatoes of your choice.

Pig kidneys in white wine

Delicious with watercress and pureed potatoes.

Ingredients for 4

4 pig kidneys
8oz/250g button mushrooms
A pinch of thyme
2 glasses of East Anglian white wine
2oz/60g butter
1 large garlic clove, crushed
1 dessertspoon flour
Plenty of chopped parsley
Salt and freshly ground pepper

Skin the kidneys and cube, removing white core. Melt the butter in a large frying pan. As soon as it starts bubbling add the meat and garlic. Stir well until the meat starts taking colour. Add the mushrooms, stir for a further 3 minutes, sprinkle with flour, stir once more. Now add wine, thyme, salt and pepper. Turn the heat down and cook, uncovered, for 20 minutes. Serve with a sprinkling of fresh chopped parsley.
NB. This is an excellent mixture to serve inside vol-au-vent cases.

Liver with apples

Ingredients for 4

8 very thin slices of pig's liver
4 thin rashers of oak-smoked streaky bacon
1 onion, chopped
3oz/90g butter
Salt and pepper
2 cooking apples
1 small garlic clove, crushed
1 measure of port

Cut the liver in small cubes, slice the bacon and saute them both with the chopped onion in 2oz/60g of butter. When the meat has taken colour, season with pepper and salt, add the glass of port and a little warm water. Cook gently, uncovered, for 20 minutes. In the meantime, peel, core and slice the apples. Saute them in the remaining butter until golden and soft. Serve on the same plate as the liver.

Potted pork

A very mild preparation. It is very good on toast or with bread and salad.

Ingredients

4lbs/2kg belly of pork
2oz/60g butcher's lard
1 teaspoon thyme
A pinch of mace
Plenty of salt and pepper
1 glass of East Anglian white wine
Water

Use a large, heavy flameproof casserole dish. Remove the rind from the meat and place in the pan with salt, pepper, thyme and mace. Cube the lard and dot over meat. Cover the dish and cook over very low heat, adding wine and a little water after 30 minutes. There should be, at all stages of cooking, enough liquid in the dish for the meat not to attach or colour, but at no stage should the meat 'swim' in liquid. Cook for 2 to 3 hours, until the meat is so tender you can shred it with a fork. Check seasoning. Shred the meat and pound it inside a preserve jar. Pour a little melted lard on the top, leave to cool in a cold place and wait at least 24 hours before eating. Always serve very chilled.

Lincolnshire brawn

A light, summer cold meat. Serve it with a tossed green salad. For extra flavour, slice the meat, arrange it on a serving dish and spoon a mixture of oil, vinegar, chopped parsley, tarragon and chives, salt and pepper over the slices. Do this 1 hour before serving the meat. The flavours will blend; it is really good.

Ingredients

1 pig's head
4 pig's tongue
10 Lincolnshire sausages
1 onion
1 carrot
1 leek
Plenty of salt and pepper
1 glass of vinegar
Water

Soak the pig's head and tongues overnight in water and vinegar. The following day, rinse well and place in a large pan with herbs, carrot, onion and leek. Cover with water, bring to the boil, skin the surface once or twice, then cook, partly covered until meat falls off the bones.

Lift the meat and vegetables from the stock and, while you remove bones and skin from head and tongues, poach the sausages in the stock. Cut all the meat including the sausages, when cooked, in small cubes. Adjust seasoning – the whole thing should be highly seasoned.

Place meat and sausages in a mould, reduce the stock until it thickens, pour some over the meat. Press down with a weight. Leave for 24 hours before eating.

* * * * *

A recipe book on pork was compiled by Pauls Agriculture of Ipswich, last year. The wives of British pig producers were invited to enter a competition and the winning recipes, from all over Britain, are listed in the 'Pauls British Pig Meat Recipe Book'. I have pleasure, with the kind permission of Pauls Agriculture, in including the winner's recipe from Mrs Y. Woollard, Essex as well as some others from the East Anglian region.

Roast pork with walnut and spinach stuffing

(Mrs Y. Woollard, Essex)

Ingredients for 8

3lb/1kg piece spare rib of pork
4oz/120g spinach
1oz/30g butter
1 onion, chopped
3oz/90g cooked rice
2oz/60g chopped walnuts
1 egg
1 tablespoon double cream
Salt and pepper

Heat the oven to 350F, 180C, gas mark 4. Make stuffing i.e. wash the spinach, take out any stalks. Place in pan, cook for 2 minutes or until soft. Drain well and chop. Keep hot. Melt butter in small pan, add chopped onion and cook for 5 mins. Add the chopped bacon and fry quickly. Remove from heat. Stir in all other ingredients, including spinach and mix well. Stuff the piece of pork and tie into shape with string. Roast in oven for about 2 hours or until juices run clear. Frozen spinach can be used.

Suggestion for vegetables: Lemon carrots, parsnip balls, Duchesse potatoes.

Meatloaf

(M. A. K. Middleton, Norfolk)

Ingredients

2lb/1kg minced lean pork
2 eggs
3 fluid oz milk
7 fluid oz single cream
3 teaspoons salt
White pepper to taste
1 tablespoon margarine
¾lb/370g celery
4oz/120g smoked ham
½oz herb soft cheese

Set oven to 425F, 220C, gas mark 7. Mix minced pork, salt, eggs, milk and ¾ of the cream. Slice celery very finely. Divide the minced pork in two halves and flatten out on greaseproof paper. Put ham and celery mixed, on the middle of each piece. Roll up like a swiss roll. Put on baking tray. Mix the cheese with the rest of the cream. Pour over the loaves. Bake in the oven without basting for 40 minutes. Serve with potato gratin.

BACON, HAM AND PORK PRODUCTS

Breakfast of ham and hot buttered pears

Choose a firm, late season pear for a very unusual autumn or winter breakfast. Rather than sugar, I bake the pears in Copella pear and apple juice

Ingredients for 4

2 large pears
2oz/60g unsalted butter
1 large glass of Copella pear and apple juice
Freshly ground black pepper
A touch of cinnamon
A little lemon juice

Preheat the oven to 425F, 220C, gas mark 7

Peel and core the pears. Cut them in regular slices. Place them in a shallow dish with the pear and apple juice. Sprinkle with a little cinnamon. Dot the pears with butter, grind fresh pepper over them and bake in oven until tender. Serve warm with thick slices of East Anglian ham and plenty of hot buttered granary bread.

Gammon en croute with cheese stuffing

(Mrs W. R. Wingfield, Norfolk – The Pauls British Pig Meat Recipe Book)

Ingredients

5oz/125g cheese
3oz/90g breadcrumbs
Pepper
1 egg
2 – 3lb/1 – 1½kg cold cooked gammon
1lb/500g puff pastry

Make the stuffing: Mix breadcrumbs, grated cheese, pepper and enough beaten egg to bind. Trim any fat from gammon and cut in half horizontally. Press the stuffing over one half, replace second piece of gammon on top. Roll out pastry large enough to enclose the gammon.

Trim edges and make into pastry leaves. Brush edges with beaten egg and fold around the gammon. Place on baking tray, seam down. Pierce top, decorate with pastry leaves, leave in refrigerator for 30 minutes. Glaze with egg and bake for 40 minutes covering with foil to prevent over-browning. Serve hot or cold.

Norfolk ham and mushroom dumplings

Smooth potato dumplings to be served with plenty of melted butter, Norwich 'hot peas' or pureed spinach.

Ingredients for 12 dumplings

6 medium potatoes
2 eggs
2 egg yolks
1 tablespoon flour
3 thick slices of ham
¼lb/120g button mushrooms
2 small onions
1oz/30g butter
Some flour for final preparation.

Boil the potatoes, mash them and leave to cool. Dice the ham and mushrooms, chop the onions very finely. Fry these three ingredients in butter until the onions have softened. Set aside to cool.

Combine potatoes, eggs, egg yolks and flour. Shape potato mixture into 12 balls. Make an indentation into each potato ball with your thumb. Fill with 2 teaspoons of ham mixture. Reshape the potato balls, roll into flour. Drop in boiling water, a few at a time. When the dumplings rise, remove with a slotted spoon. Drain well and serve with the melted butter.

Potted ham

An ideal way to make use of an end of ham. It will keep for a while and is good on toast.

1½lb/750g ham
6oz/180g unsalted butter
A small spoonful of ground mace and nutmeg
A little cayenne pepper

Remove rind and fat from the ham. Cut in chunks and combine all the ingredients in a food blender. Press into potting jars, cover with a little clarified butter and keep in a cold room.

Ham and mushroom bake

This is a good snack with pureed potatoes and a green salad

Ingredients for 4

4 thin slices of ham
½lb/250g button mushrooms
1 large onion, chopped
1oz/30g butter
4 tablespoons thick cream
1 tablespoon tomato puree
4oz/120g grated cheese
Black pepper to taste
A dash of Worcestershire sauce

Warm oven to 450°F, 230°C, gas mark 8

Gently cook the chopped onion in butter until transparent. Spoon on to the base of a baking dish. Now saute the mushrooms, sliced, in the same frying pan as the onions. Divide the mushrooms in 4 portions and spoon in the centre of each ham slice. Roll the ham slices and lay them, seam down, in the baking dish. Mix the cream together with the tomato puree, Worcestershire sauce and pepper. Spoon over the ham rolls, sprinkle with grated cheese and bake in the hot oven for 20 minutes.

Lincolnshire stuffed chine

An ancient recipe, so easy to reproduce now that all herbs are freshly available. The bacon chine, a cured shoulder of pork, is stuffed, steamed and eaten cold, often with cold fowl. It is the great speciality of Lincolnshire.

Soak the chine overnight in cold water. The following day, pat dry and cut through the meat in spaces of about ¾ inch. Fill the nicks made by the cutting with a mixture of fresh herbs and ground black pepper. The herbs should include: parsley, chives, marjoram, fresh thyme, lettuce, English mace, lovage and chervil. Tie a cloth around the chine and steam for 2 to 3 hours according to size.

This cold meat is excellent with any of the Culpeper herb jellies, or home-made quince jelly (see recipe page 90)

SAUSAGES & BLACK PUDDING

I found lots of those when I visited Bryan Pickering at his shop in Old Costessey, near Norwich. From Grandad's recipe to smoked and spicy, his selection of ten or so kinds of sausages are all home prepared without colouring, preservatives of artificial flavouring. The black pudding is deliciously light and fluffy and has won an award. Even better, Bryan Pickering has won this year the title of Retail Butcher of the Year, at a London held competition. I am not surprised – he has immense flair and will turn the plainest of meat cut into something special, from belly of pork to the most expensive cut of veal. He is one of these people with a total culinary instinct.

Two of Bryan's own recipes are to be found in the book, but, in the meantime, let's see what could be done with the Pickering's or other good East Anglian sausages and black pudding.

Black pudding and mushroom bap

My favourite snack, rich in taste, well balanced by the mustard and watercress.

Ingredients for 2 baps

½ a black pudding
¼lb/120g button mushrooms
2 soft baps
1 dessertspoon port
A large knob of butter
Colman's horseradish mustard powder
Watercress

Skin and slice the black pudding, slice the mushrooms. Melt the butter in a frying pan and, as soon as it froths, saute the black pudding slices until they take colour on both sides. Add the mushrooms, port, salt and pepper and cook, uncovered, for a few minutes. Mix 1 teaspoon of Colman's horseradish mustard powder to a paste, spread on the opened bap. Top with freshly washed watercress. Spoon the hot mixture over the watercress. Eat at once.

East Anglian winter pie

A pork pie, mysteriously seasoned by the flavour of black pudding and cooking apples. I like to make it with the old fashioned lard pie crust, but any fat can be used.

Ingredients for 4 or 6

1lb/500g lean pork pieces
¼lb/120g smoked streaky bacon pieces
6oz/180g black pudding
2 onions, chopped
2 cooking apples
4 juniper berries
Chopped parsley and thyme
¼pt/⅛ litre of good chicken stock mixed with a glass of East Anglian dry wine

For the pastry
8oz/250g flour
5oz/150g lard
A pinch of salt
Water

Make pastry: Rub a little of the lard into the flour in a basin. Add salt and enough water to form a stiff dough. Transfer to a floured pastry board and roll it out with a floured rolling pin. Lay small knobs of lard dented into the pastry in alternate rows all over the surface. Sprinkle with a little flour and fold over the edges all round until they meet in the middle. Turn the pastry over on the board and roll it again. Repeat the spreading of lard and roll for a third time to the thickness required.

Take a 2pt/1 litre pie dish. Remove the rind from bacon pieces. Peel, core and chop the apples. Peel and chop the onions. Skin and dice the black pudding. Place the ingredients in any order inside pie dish with the meat. Sprinkle with herbs. Pour stock mixed with wine over the meat. Wet the edge of the pie dish and lay a border of pastry around it. Moisten the pastry border, cover the dish with pastry, cut even all round, pinch the edges and decorate with pastry leaves. Make a hole in the centre and glaze with the beaten yolk of an egg or a little milk.

Bake in hot oven (425F, 220C, gas mark 7) for 20 minutes, then lower the heat to 350F, 180C gas mark 4 and continue baking for 1½ hours. Cover the pastry with foil or greaseproof paper if the pastry takes too much colour. Eat warm with green vegetable and carrots.

Savoury truffles

To be served warm with roast white meat or fowl.

Ingredients

½lb/250g minced pork	**A pinch of dry mustard**
½lb/250g black pudding	**One beaten egg**
1oz/30g chopped hazelnuts	**1tsp of chives, chopped finely**

Skin the black pudding, and using a fork or a food blender mash all the ingredients together. With floured hands turn the mixture into small balls. Roast for 15 minutes around the meat towards the end of cooking time, or fry separately in a little butter of lard.

Baked sausages with white wine and tomatoes

Breakfast type sausages are not recommended for this dish – they need to be very meaty. Serve as a main course with either pureed or sauteed potatoes, a green salad and plenty of mustard.

Ingredients for 4

2 sausages per person	**1 small glass of East Anglian white wine**
2 onions	**Pepper and salt to taste**
4 tomatoes	

Preheat the oven to 450°F, 230°C, gas mark 8

Grease the bottom of an ovenproof dish with a little oil. Peel and slice the onions, lay them inside the dish. Now lay the sausages, side by side, surrounded by the tomatoes cut in half. Bake in the hot oven for 20 minutes. Five minutes before the end of cooking, spoon out excess fat and pour the wine over the dish. Serve very hot.

Beef & Lamb

Beef & Lamb

Due to the transformation of the land, mostly turned into large arable cropping, and the relatively dry climate which does not always help the quality of grassland, beef and lamb still take second place in East Anglia compared with pork or even poultry.

But with the efforts of local farmers and the constant guidance of the Meat and Livestock Commission in the area, the situation has improved a great deal within the last ten years. The East Anglian butchers I met while researching this book assure me that local beef is readily available in their shops all year round and lamb when in season.

It is a comforting thought both for the butcher and his customer. It means that the quality is there, the cuts can be discussed – it makes a big difference to the final result of a main course.

As for the wine – although some red wine can now be found in East Anglia, I have never disassociated white or rose wine with the cooking of red meat – very often it creates a much lighter sauce without impairing the taste of the ingredients.

So, once again, the two East Anglian products complement each other.

Lincolnshire beef soup

As the meat is served in the soup, this is more a lunchtime or evening snack than a first course. Follow it with a good local fruit tart.

Ingredients for 6

1lb shin of beef, diced
1 small middle piece of marrow bone
1 head of celery
2 leeks
2 carrots
2 onions
1 small parsnip
1 small turnip
A glass of East Anglian wine
1 bayleaf
2 sprigs of thyme
A few blackpeppercorns
Ground seasalt
3pt/1½ litre of water

Place the meat and marrow bone in a large pan, cover with the water and bring slowly to the boil. Skim the surface two or three times. Now add the vegetables cut in chunks, bring to the boil, skim once more if necessary, lower the heat, cover the pan and simmer gently for 2 hours. Twenty minutes before serving, add the wine, bring to the boil, and cook uncovered to slightly reduce and therefore thicken the stock. Serve the broth together with meat and vegetables without putting the soup through a blender.

Norwich Monday beef

Ingredients for 4

2lbs/1kg large fresh garden peas
2 lettuce hearts
4 spring onions
1 teaspoon horseradish mustard
2 teaspoons Worcestershire sauce
½pt/¼litre stock, made with beef gravy
Slices of cold roast beef
1oz/30g butter rolled in flour

Put the peas, lettuce hearts, spring onions and stock in a pan. Cover and simmer slowly for 1 hour. Add the sliced cold meat, season with plenty of freshly ground pepper, simmer gently for another hour. Stir in the mustard and Worcestershire sauce, the butter, in small pieces. Mix well and serve at once with plenty of bread.

Boiled beef and sea salt

Salt has had a bad name in dietary circles in the last few years. As long as it is not taken to excess, it is important to understand that the human body would not function properly without salt: muscles would not work, nerves would not carry messages, food would remain undigested. Those facts were brought home when I visited the fascinating Maldon Crystal Salt Company.

The creeks and inlets of the Essex coast are probably the saltiest stretches of water in England. For centuries, the completely natural and unadulterated product has been prepared in Maldon. It is exported to many countries and can be found all over Britain through the chemists and health food shops.

Beef and salt have lived together for many years: salt beef, once a necessary way of keeping the meat, is now a delicacy. And corned beef, of course, owes its name to the salt granules or 'corns' used in its manufacturing.

Maldon boiled beef with puree of broad beans

Ingredients for 4

1 piece of topside or silverside	**2 cloves**
1 carrot	**A few peppercorns**
1 onion	**Water**
1 leek	**3lbs/1½kg fresh broad beans**
A bunch of herbs	**Maldon Crystal salt**

Peel the onion and insert the two cloves. Wash leek carefully and place it with the piece of meat and all the other ingredients in a pan. Cover with water, bring to the boil, skim once or twice and simmer until the meat is cooked and tender. Shell the broad beans and remove outer skin. You will be left with the delicious vegetable which purees as it cooks.

Lift the meat off the stock. Make a soup for a first course by blending the cooking vegetables with the stock. Serve the beef, hot and sliced, with the puree of broad beans mixed with a little butter and the seasalt. Grind plenty of seasalt over each slice of meat (salt was not included in the boiling of the meat). Eat with the vegetable and no other seasoning – it really creates an individual taste.

Potted beef

Ingredients

4lbs/2kg lean stewing beef
5oz/150g unsalted butter
1 little mace
1 bayleaf
1 clove
1 onion
1 glass East Anglian white wine
2 glasses of water
Freshly ground pepper and seasalt

Peel the onion and insert the clove in it. Place the meat in a heavy, flameproof pot. Add water and wine and the bayleaf. Simmer very gently for at least 2 hours until the meat is very cooked. Add a little water when necessary. When done, remove onion and bayleaf and transfer the meat, in pieces, to an electric mincer. Mince and season well with freshly ground seasalt, pepper and mace. When it has reached a thick paste consistency, mix in some clarified butter and a little cooking stock if any. Press into pots, pour butter over the top of each. Cover and keep in a cold room.

East Anglian pressed beef

A good summer or picnic main course. Serve it with a herby potato salad and a large mixed salad. Don't forget East Anglian mustard or horseradish as a condiment!

Ingredients

2lbs/1kg chuck steak
1 pig's trotter
A bunch of herbs
¼ bottle of East Anglian white wine
1 onion
1 clove
1 large carrot
Salt and pepper to taste.

Peel the onion, insert the clove, place all the ingredients in a heavy flameproof casserole dish and season with salt and pepper. Simmer over very low heat, adding a little water if necessary until the meat is well cooked. When cooked, lift the meat and carrot from the stock. Slice the carrot in regular slices and lay in a pattern at the bottom of a mould. Cut the meat coarsely and press it on top of the carrots. Reduce the stock by boiling for a few minutes, strain it through a nylon sieve and pour over the meat. Adjust seasoning, cover and cool in the refrigerator for 24 hours before eating.

Turn on to a serving dish by placing the mould in warm water for a few seconds. Slice and decorate with a few lettuce leaves.

East Anglian pressed beef with celeriac

If you do not wish to eat the pressed beef cold, here is a good recipe for a luncheon.

Ingredients for 4

1 small celeriac
4 thick slices of pressed beef
Bottled or tinned crushed tomatoes
1 handful of fresh breadcrumbs
4oz/120g of grated cheese
A few knobs of butter
Pepper and salt

Peel the celeriac, divide it into 4 thick slices and cook in boiling water until just tender. In the meantime, preheat the oven to 425F, 220C, gas mark 7. Drain the celeriac and alternate slices of beef and celeriac in a baking dish. Cover with the crushed tomatoes, salt and pepper, the breadcrumbs and grated cheese mixed. Place in the oven for 20 minutes. Eat with a green salad and crusty bread.

Lincoln salad

Ingredients for 4

2 slices of East Anglian pressed beef, cold
1 firm lettuce
1 bunch watercress
1 beetroot
4 tablespoons cooked peas
4 tablespoons cooked and diced potatoes
1 tablespoon capers
2 to 3 tablespoons of mayonnaise or
Oil and vinegar dressing.

Wash the lettuce and watercress and chop, reserving a few good lettuce leaves. Peel and dice the beetroot and reserve for decoration. Cube the meat. Blend all ingredients except beetroot with mayonnaise or dressing. Arrange the lettuce leaves at the bottom of a salad bowl. Pile the salad on them and garnish with the diced beetroot.

Beef and iceberg lettuce parcels

One of the most recent products of East Anglia, the iceberg lettuce bears large outer leaves. Wrapped around meat, tomatoes, onions and herbs it makes a delicious main course. Serve with new potatoes and buttered carrots.

Ingredients for 4

1lb/500g lean ground beef
4 large iceberg lettuce outer leaves
Lettuce heart
6 tomatoes, peeled
4 rashers of smoked streaky bacon
2 medium size onions
2 basil leaves
1 glass East Anglian white wine
¼pt/⅛ litre chicken stock

Chop the lettuce heart, chop the peeled tomatoes, peel and chop 2 onions. Combine with the ground beef, salt and pepper and chopped basil. Divide in 4 portions and spoon at the centre of each outside leaf. Fold the lettuce onto itself, wrap a bacon rasher around each parcel, secure if necessary with either a wooden skewer or some string. Place in shallow ovenproof dish, pour wine and chicken stock over lettuce parcels, cover with foil and bake in preheated oven (400F, 200C, gas mark 6) for 30 minutes.

Huntingdon celebration rib

A large piece of boned rib of beef wrapped round a succulent stuffing of East Anglian vegetables and ham. Make the stuffing and, for this very special dish, ask you butcher to insert it in the meat – it can be a little tricky to prepare at home.

Ingredients for 8

4lbs/2kg boneless rib of beef
4oz/120g ham
1 carrot
1 onion
¼lb/120g dwarf beans
¼lb/120g peas
1 small parsnip
1 clove of garlic
1 teaspoon of chopped fresh parsley
½ teaspoon chopped fresh thyme
2 basil leaves
1 teaspoon of tarragon
½ teaspoon chives
1 egg
Butter
4oz/120g thick cream
1 tablespoon East Anglian white wine
1 teaspoon brandy
Freshly ground salt and pepper

Clean, peel and dice all the vegetables as small as possible. Chop the herbs together. Melt some butter in a frying pan and as soon as it starts bubbling, stir in all the vegetables. Lower the heat and cook for 8 to 10 minutes. Transfer to a mixing bowl and leave to cool. Add the crushed garlic. Mince the ham or cut in fine strips. When the vegetables have cooled blend in ham, egg and cream. Add wine and brandy. Season freely – this stuffing needs to be well spiced to enhance the flavour of the vegetables. Chill for 1 hour.

Stuff the meat, secure with string without crushing the stuffing too much. Roast as usual. Serve with roast potatoes, leaf spinach or cabbage and a dish of sauteed cup mushrooms.

Ox tongue with pickled samphire sauce

Serve with mashed potatoes

Ingredients for the tongue

1 ox tongue
A bunch of herbs
Peppercorns
1 carrot
2 onions
1 clove

Soak tongue overnight in plenty of cold water. Change the water once if possible. Place the tongue in a large saucepan together with other ingredients. Bring to the boil then simmer gently for 2½ hours. Lift the meat from the stock. Skin the tongue, slice on to a serving dish and keep warm while making the sauce.

For the sauce

2 oz/60g butter
1 tablespoon flour
A small glass East Anglian white wine
2 tablespoons pickled samphire tips
1 tablespoon of capers
A pinch of mace
Black pepper to taste.

Melt butter and flour in a saucepan, stirring well. Add some stock, little by little to avoid lumps, until you have the required quantity of sauce. Add the wine, pepper and condiments and cook for a further 6 to 8 minutes. Pour some sauce over the tongue. Pass the rest round in a gravyboat.

LAMB

Herb garden breast of lamb

A few Fenmen still bear the name of their origin: Flanders. So it is with Flanders Hopkin who, with his wife Leonita runs a herb nursery from his grandfather's old house at Queen Adelaide, near Ely. They have managed to give an air of kept wilderness to the whole garden – it is enchanting and probably more difficult to achieve than growing plants in orderly rows. There is, of course, an Elizabethan knot-garden, but the herbs can also be found around the large pond, under trees or over paths. Leonita has a great understanding of the relationship between herbs and primary products, and her recipes are not kept secret.

Ingredients for 4

1 boned breast of lamb
A little butter
4oz/120g breadcrumbs
4oz/120g sausage meat
1 onion, chopped
½ teaspoon of PennyRoyal
½ teaspoon hyssop
Salt and pepper

Preheat the oven to 400F, 200C, gas mark 6

Make stuffing with breadcrumbs, sausagemeat and herbs. Spoon it in the pocket of a lean breast of lamb. Roll and tie the meat. Roast with a little butter for 1½ hours. Eat cold with a tossed salad of crisp lettuce and mixed fresh herbs.

Lamb and leek bake

(A recipe adapted from Jill Norris' book 'The Winter Warmth'.)

Ingredients for 4

8oz/250g chopped onions
1 garlic clove, crushed
Butter or oil
1½lb/750g lean minced beef
1lb/500g leeks
2 tablespoons tomato puree
3 fluid oz. East Anglian white wine
1 teaspoon ground cinnamon
1 teaspoon chopped parsley
Salt and pepper to taste.

Fry onions and garlic in butter or oil, add the meat and fry lightly. Clean leeks, slice them and blanch for 2 minutes in boiling salted water. Mix together the tomato puree, wine, cinnamon, salt and pepper and parsley. Pour over meat, stir well and simmer for a short time. Using a lightly greased ovenproof deep dish, spread a layer of the leeks on the bottom of the dish and cover with a layer of lamb. Repeat, making sure you end with a layer of meat. Cover with foil and bake in moderate oven for 30 minutes.

In the meantime make the following topping: blend together 2 level tablespoons of flour, 2 eggs, 1 egg yolk, ¾ pint of natural yogurt, 2oz grated cheddar, seasoning and ½ teaspoon nutmeg. Pour this mixture over the bake and place, uncovered in the oven for a further 30 minutes, or until golden.

Bryan Pickering's breast of lamb

Ingredients

1 English breast of lamb, boned and trimmed
½lb/250g lean mince beef
1 Bramley apple
4oz/120g shelled walnuts
½ egg white
Salt and pepper

Mix mince beef, egg white, salt and pepper well in bowl until sticky. Peel and core apple, chop into small pieces and add with walnuts to the minced beef. Lay breast of lamb on flat board, spread the stuffing and secure with string. Bake in a moderate oven 325F, 170C, gas mark 3 for approximately 1 hour.

Salt marsh leg of lamb

The taste of salt marsh lamb is succulent. The piquancy of samphire and caper sauce is the ideal accompaniment.

Ingredients for 6

1 leg of lamb
2oz/60g butter
2 dessertspoons flour
2pts/1 litre chicken stock
1 glass East Anglian white wine
2 tablespoons pickled samphire tips
2 tablespoons capers
Salt and pepper to taste
1 carrot
1 onion
A bunch of fresh herbs
18 small new potatoes, peeled

Place the meat in a large stewpan together with carrot and onion, herbs, chicken stock and black pepper. Bring to the boil, skim once or twice and cook slowly for 20 minutes per pound. Twenty minutes before end of cooking time, add the peeled potatoes. Lift meat and potatoes from the stock and keep warm while you make the sauce: Melt butter, add flour stirring well. Now add slowly ½pt/¼ litre of meat stock, stirring constantly to avoid lumps. Add the white wine, capers and samphire. Adjust seasoning and simmer for 10 minutes.

Slice the meat, surround with potatoes. Spoon the sauce over meat and vegetables and serve.

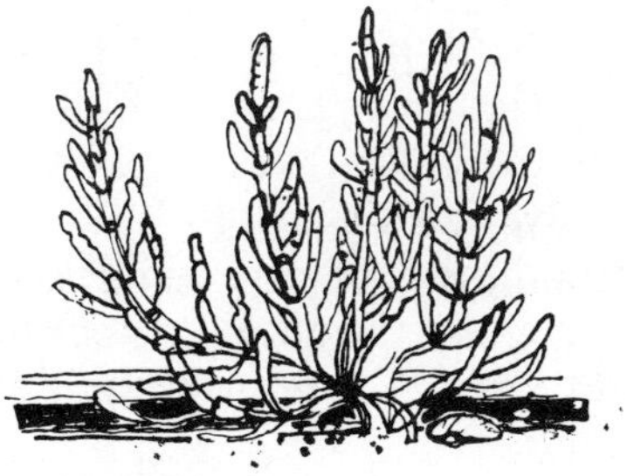

Braised shoulder of lamb with turnips

A fine combination of the first spring purple turnips and a shoulder of spring lamb.

Ingredients for 6

1 shoulder of lamb
1lb/500g small turnips
2 onions
1 clove of garlic (optional)
Salt and pepper
1 glass of water

Preheat the oven to 425°F, 220°C, gas mark 7

Wash the turnips but do not peel them. Peel the onions. Place the sliced turnips and onions at the base of a baking dish. Lay the meat over the vegetables, season with salt and pepper. Add the glass of water and cook for 2 hours, lowering the oven heat after the first 45 minutes. Baste frequently. Serve with the turnips as garnish.

Summer lamb with courgettes and lemon

For a summer's day luncheon, serve with a bowl of new potatoes with herby butter and a chilled bottle of white or rose East Anglian wine.

Ingredients for 4

1 shoulder of lamb, very lean
2oz/60g butter
¼pt/⅛ litre chicken stock
1 lemon
8oz/250g courgettes
A few tarragon leaves
Chopped parsley
Pepper to taste

Ask your butcher to bone and roll the shoulder of lamb with the tarragon leaves. Using a heavy, flameproof casserole dish, brown the meat on all sides in butter, add seasoning and chicken stock. Cover and simmer for 1½ hours, basting the meat frequently with the stock.

Slice the courgettes without peeling them. Peel the lemon and divide in segments. Arrange the courgettes and lemon segments around the meat, cover and cook over gentle heat for a further 30 minutes. Lift the meat from the stock and the courgette and lemon with a slotted spoon. Arrange on a hot serving dish. Reduce the stock for the sauce. Pour over meat and courgettes, sprinkle with chopped parsley. Serve with quarters of fresh lemon.

Vegetables & Salads

Vegetables & salads

The production of vegetables is by any yardstick a major industry in East Anglia. The entire region produces more than a third of the country's vegetables, including a third of the pea crop, half the onions and two thirds of all the carrots grown in Britain. Potatoes and root vegetables are grown on a very large scale and Lincolnshire is the undisputed leader in the production of brassicas.

The smallholding and glasshouse products from the region's market gardeners provide all the classic salad vegetables and in recent years many producers have had great success with less indigenous plants such as celeriac, radicchio, chicory, endive and obscure varieties of lettuce.

The small green Norfolk asparagus is justifiably the pride of the county.

Most cottages have at least one devoted gardener. And people like John and Caroline Stevens, owners of Suffolk Herbs, are fighting the anomalous EEC rules, from dawn to dusk, to try to stop the extinction of old traditional vegetables like the Oakey Onion, the Painted Lady Runner Bean, or the Cottager's Kale.

It is therefore not surprising that the British Quality Vegetable and Salad Association has its headquarters in the picturesque town of Louth in Lincolnshire. And no wonder that some farmers, after a lifetime of hard work, proudly carry local nicknames such as 'the Carrot King' or 'the Mushroom Magnate'.

It is extremely pleasing to find local, seasonal vegetables on the menu in most East Anglian restaurants and in Norwich, Lynton Johnson this year opened one of the best and most attractive vegetarian restaurants I have ever visited. No nut cutlets, no beansprouts feeding themselves in the cracks of pine tables which have seen better days. Instead a clean, cool decor and a varied and interesting menu prepared daily by the cook Yvonne Morris, using fresh local products. It is The Mecca, at 5 Orford Hill, Norwich. The restaurant is licensed, with a good few local wines in the list, and I would defy any confirmed non-vegetarian to dislike a meal there. So, with or without meat, with or without local wine, let's see what can be done with the numerous products of Britain's eastern kitchen garden.

Vegetables

ASPARAGUS

Despite many varieties grown all over the region, the native small green Norfolk asparagus seems very much in demand throughout Britain these days. Probably the nearest species to the original 16th century wild asparagus, its distinctive taste has no equal. As it is thin it also has the advantage of cooking very quickly and therefore keeps all of its natural goodness. When young, it can even be enjoyed raw in salads. The most popular way of eating asparagus is of course with melted butter, sometimes flavoured with a little lemon juice.

It is also a great delicacy with a sauce made of a knob of melted butter and 3 tablespoons of thick cream. A few 18th or 19th century recipes are still compatible with today's diet, like the two which follow.

Asparagus loaves

This is a good lunchtime snack.

Ingredients for 4

4 individual cottage loaves (white or brown)	**2 egg yolks**
½lb/250g asparagus	**Salt and pepper**
A small jar of double cream	**Nutmeg**
	Butter

Boil and drain the asparagus keeping only the tips. Warm the bread through. Take the top off each loaf and remove the dough. Over low heat beat the egg yolks with the cream, stirring well until the mixture thickens. Mix in half the asparagus tips, add seasoning and nutmeg. Spoon the mixture inside each loaf. Top with the remaining asparagus tips carefully arranged, pour a little melted butter over the top and serve at once with freshly ground black pepper.

Asparagus pudding

A very delicate first course. Serve with melted butter and toast fingers.

Ingredients

½lb/250g of asparagus
2 dessertspoons of minced ham
4 eggs
A little milk
1 dessertspoon of flour
A few tarragon leaves
Salt and pepper
A knob of butter

Mince ham very finely and mix it with four well-beaten eggs, flour, salt and pepper and a knob of butter the size of a walnut. Cut the top part of the asparagus into very small pieces and blend with other ingredients. Now add enough milk to give the mixture a thick creamy consistency. Pour it into a well buttered mould or pudding basin, wrap in foil and steam in a large saucepan for 2 hours. When done, turn onto a serving dish and pour some melted butter round it.

Chilled asparagus

A pleasant first course for a hot day.

Boil or steam the asparagus leaving it slightly crunchy. Chill for at least 2 hours in the refrigerator. Serve in individual dishes with single cream chilled and mixed with a few tablespoons of cold chicken stock, chopped chives and chervil with a dash of lemon juice. Sprinkle with a little Cayenne pepper. Eat with fresh crusty bread.

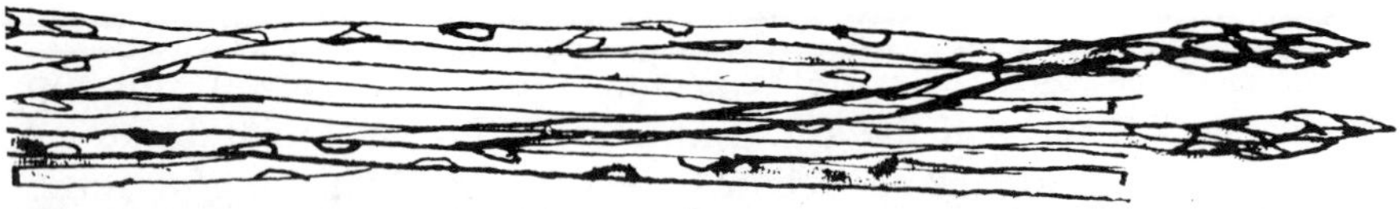

Asparagus, pea and mushroom casserole

To be eaten on its own or as a vegetable with fowl or white meat

Ingredients for 4

½lb/250g asparagus	**2oz/30g butter**
4 outer leaves of lettuce	**1 teaspoon of chopped chervil**
½lb/250g young peas	**1oz/30g blanched almonds**
2 spring onions	**1 glass of strong chicken stock**
½lb/250g small button mushrooms	**Salt and pepper to taste**

Wash and chop the lettuce roughly. Chop white and green of spring onions. Place in a saucepan with lettuce, chicken stock and half the butter. Cover and simmer for 6 minutes. The lettuce leaves will melt and add flavour to the stock. Shell the peas and cut the asparagus, keeping only the tender tips. Add to saucepan, bring to the boil and simmer until nearly tender. Six minutes before the end of cooking add the small button mushrooms, whole, and the almonds. Check seasoning, cook uncovered to reduce the stock, thicken with the rest of the butter and serve at once.

Asparagus soup

This soup can be eaten warm, served with pieces of bite-size fried bread or, for a refreshing summer first course, can be served iced.

Ingredients for 4 to 6

1lb/500g asparagus	**A small pot of single cream**
2 pints/1 litre good chicken stock	**A little white pepper**

Cook the asparagus in the chicken stock. Keep one tip per person for decoration. Liquidise, check seasoning. To serve hot, pour cream in the soup and stir over a gentle heat for a few minutes. To serve iced: Place the liquidised soup in the refrigerator for at least 2 hours. Serve with a teaspoon of iced cream on each serving. Decorate with remaining tips in both cases.

BEETROOT

Autumn Appetiser

Grated raw beetroot is excellent. Mix it with plenty of lambs lettuce, a grated shallot, a few walnut kernels, a few thin slices of Cox's apple. Dress it with apple juice, lemon and oil and sprinkle with chervil or parsley before serving.

Beetroot and spinach mould

Make in individual ramequin dishes. A deep green lining of spinach filled with beetroot, it is as visual as delectable. A splendid garnish for roast pork or goose.

Boil beetroot in salted water until tender. Peel, dice finely and season with butter salt and black pepper. Set aside. Blanch large spinach leaves. Drain well. Line well buttered ramequins with the spinach leaves, using enough to make quite a thick lining. Press in the beetroot pieces. Keep warm in a bain-marie while you make the sauce.

Ingredients for the sauce

1 small pot of sour cream	**A touch of Cayenne pepper**
½ teaspoon grated spring onion	**A little ground mace**
Salt and pepper	**A knob of butter**

Mix together in a saucepan and heat slowly. Turn the moulds onto plates and spoon a little sauce over each one. To eat as a vegetarian dish, add a few chopped walnuts and hazelnuts to the beetroot.

BEANS

Boston (England) beans

Just for fun, in memory of the Pilgrim Fathers and to surprise the next American visitors, let's have our own Boston Beans.

Ingredients for 4 to 6

1lb/500g shelled broad beans	**2 glasses of chicken stock**
1lb/500g peeled tomatoes	**1oz/30g butter**
6oz/180g bacon pieces	**A few savory leaves**
1 glass East Anglian white wine	**Chopped parsley**
1 large onion, chopped	**Pepper to taste**

First make a fresh tomato sauce as follows: melt the butter in a frying pan and, when it froths, add the bacon pieces and the chopped onion. Stir well until golden grown, add the peeled tomatoes cut in large chunks, the chicken stock and white wine. Season with pepper and savory and leave to simmer, uncovered until the liquid reduces by half and the mixture takes a good sauce consistency. Boil the broad beans until tender. Drain well and fold into the sauce. Serve on its own or with meat garnished with chopped parsley.

BROCCOLI

Suffolk Brunch

Freshly boiled or steamed broccoli, fine rashers of grilled sweet-cured bacon and poached eggs, served with a melted butter with herbs. Delicious with walnut brown bread (see recipe page 168)

Ingredients per person

1 broccoli spear	**A little freshly ground sea salt**
1 egg	**Finely chopped chervil**
1 large rasher of sweet cured bacon	**Black pepper to taste**
	A touch of lemon juice

For the butter
1oz/30g unsalted butter

Boil the broccoli for 8 to 10 minutes – it should stay quick firm. Grill the bacon, poach the egg. Place the broccoli, well drained over a bacon slice, on individual plate, add poached egg, poor on the melted butter. Serve very hot.

Broccoli and cauliflower with melted butter

Separate both vegetables in individual florets. Boil separately in salted water. Do not overcook. Lift gently off water, drain well and alternate on a serving plate. Season with the same herby butter as recipe above.

BRUSSELS SPROUTS

Lincoln sprouts

Ingredients for 4

1lb/500g small sprouts	**1oz/30g butcher's lard**
8 Lincolnshire sausages	**Salt and pepper**

Clean and wash the sprouts. Cook for 12 minutes in salted boiling water. In the meantime prick the sausages and fry them in the lard, turning occasionally to avoid burning. When cooked, keep warm. Transfer the well drained sprouts to the frying pan and stir them for 5 minutes in the pan juice. Adjust seasoning. Serve garnished with the sausages.

Holbeach bubble and squeak

Meaty haslet is made by the Swepstone family in Holbeach. Fried in a little butter with left over sprouts and potatoes, it makes a solid traditional country breakfast.

Ingredients for 4

4 slices of haslet	**1 egg**
½lb/250g cooked Brussels sprouts	**Plenty of black pepper**
½lb/250g cooked potatoes	**Butter**

Mash the two vegetables with fork. Mix with beaten egg. Fry in a good piece of butter. Fry haslet in a separate frying pan. Place in a hot dish with alternate layers of fried vegetables.

CABBAGE

Kitchen garden stuffed cabbage

Ingredients for 4

1 cabbage	**2 onions**
1lb/500g mixed vegetables	**Salt and pepper to taste**
4oz/120g butter	

Blanch the cabbage whole in boiling water for 8 minutes. Rinse under cold water and leave to cool upside down in a colander. Clean all the other vegetables (according to the season any vegetable can be used – peas, carrots, turnips, parsnips, mushrooms, broad beans, green beans are all excellent for this recipe). Chop all vegetables.

Melt half the butter in a frying pan and gently saute the vegetables. Stir constantly and cook for 6 minutes. Now open up the cabbage leaves and spoon the other vegetables in between the leaves. Fold the cabbage back and secure with string. Preheat the oven to 400F, 200C, gas mark 6. Place the cabbage in a baking dish. Add butter and a glass of water. Bake for 30 minutes. Serve with boiled potatoes.

Pureed cabbage

Excellent served with gammon steak or thick slices of East Anglian smoked ham fried in butter.

Boil and puree the cabbage with fresh butter, pepper and a touch of nutmeg. Fry the bacon or ham and pour the pan juices over the pureed cabbage, mixing well. Serve with boiled or mashed potatoes.

CAULIFLOWER

Cream of cauliflower soup

A very smooth soup – use only very white cauliflower

Ingredients for 4

1 large cauliflower
1 potato
2pts/1 litre of chicken stock
1 dessertspoon of thick cream
1 knob of butter
Streaky bacon and chopped parsley

Cook the cauliflower together with the potato in the chicken stock. Liquidise, adding cream and butter. Grill the bacon until very crisp. Chop finely. Mix with the chopped parsley and use to decorate each serving of soup.

Cauliflower souffle

Ingredients

1 cauliflower, cooked
¼pt/⅛ litre white sauce
3 egg yolks
4 egg whites
4oz/¼lb ham, minced

Preheat the oven to 350F, 180C, gas mark 4

Mash the cauliflower with a fork, blend with white sauce, beaten egg yolks and minced ham. Season. Whisk the egg white until firm, fold into the vegetable and ham mixture. Pour into a greased souffle dish, making sure it is only ¾ full. Bake for 40 to 45 minutes until well risen. Serve at once.

CARROT

Thick carrot soup

Ingredients

1lb/500g carrots
½lb/250g potatoes
1 onion, chopped
1 clove of garlic, crushed
1 teaspoon chopped tarragon
1½pt/¾ litre water
2oz/60g butter
1 dessertspoon thick cream
1 teaspoon chopped chives
Salt and pepper to taste

Place sliced carrots and potatoes in a saucepan with water, seasoning, tarragon, onion and garlic. Boil for 15 minutes. Liquidise. Return to pan, add chopped chives, butter and cream. Stir well. Serve at once.

Carrot forcemeat balls

Excellent with roast turkey, or on its own with drinks.

Ingredients

2lbs/1kg carrots, finely grated
1 onion, finely grated
4oz/¼lb mixed chopped nuts
1 egg, beaten
1 cupful breadcrumbs
Butter
2 lovage leaves, finely chopped.

Blend carrots and onion with egg, nuts, lovage, seasoning and beaten egg. Roll into balls, then in breadcrumbs. Roast for 15 minutes around the meat or fry in butter and oil and serve on its own with lemon quarters.

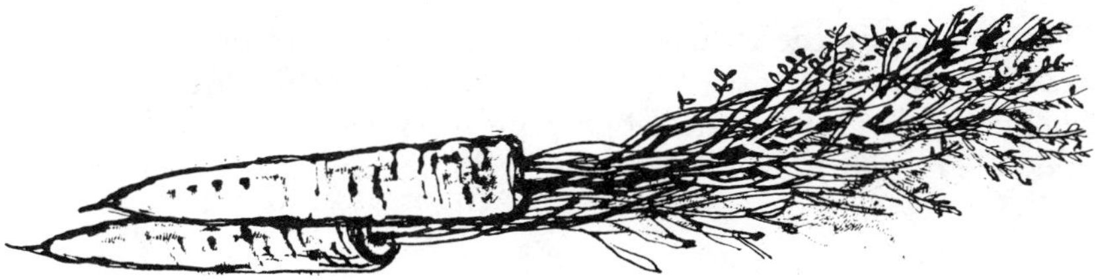

East Anglian ratatouille

A surprising taste for a summer first course, now that peppers are grown so successfully under glass in East Anglia.

Ingredients for 6

2lbs/1kg new carrots
3 green peppers
6 small pickling onions
½ teaspoon mustard
3 tablespoon oil
Lemon juice
1 garlic clove, crushed
1 teaspoon tarragon leaves

Wash and slice the carrots. Peel and half onions and cut pepper in fine strips. Using a heavy, flameproof dish, warm the oil and saute onions, carrots and peppers together. Stir until all vegetables are coated with oil. Add seasoning and tarragon. Cover and simmer over low heat for 30 minutes. When tender, add lemon juice, mix and leave to cool. Serve chilled on a large lettuce leaf. Decorate with slices of hard boiled egg.

CELERY AND CELERIAC

Celery and minted peas

Ingredients for 4

1 celery head
1lb/500g fresh peas, shelled
3 lettuce leaves
2 spring onions
Mint
Salt and pepper
A knob of butter

Wash and chop the lettuce. Place in saucepan with onions, butter, a glass of water and seasoning. Cover and simmer for 6 minutes. Add chopped celery and peas. Simmer until tender. Drain with a slotted spoon. Transfer to warm dish, toss in butter and chopped mint.

Susan's celeriac soup

It was an article in 'The Grower' magazine which decided the Spindler family to try celeriac as an autumn alternative crop, on their land, outside Newbourn, near Woodbridge. Susan Spindler says it's one of her favourite vegetable; they eat it in salads, with meat casseroles and stews and she kindly gave me her soup recipe:

Ingredients for 4

1½lb/750g celeriac
1 onion, peeled
2pts/1 litre chicken stock
Cream
Salt and pepper

Peel and roughly slice the celeriac. Place in a saucepan with chicken stock, peeled onion and seasoning. Bring to the boil and cook for 50 minutes. Liquidise and reheat with a drop of thick cream.

Supreme of East Anglian celeriac

Eat on its own with bread or as a vegetable with roast pork of chicken

Ingredients for 4

1 celeriac
1 large cooking apple
12 walnut kernels
8oz/250g smoked East Anglian streaky bacon
1 onion
1 teaspoon of chopped chives
1 tablespoon East Anglian white wine
1 small pot of double cream
Freshly grated nutmeg
Butter
Salt and pepper

Preheat the oven to 450F, 230C, gas mark 8

Peel and slice the celeriac in regular slices. Boil in salted water until tender. Par grill the bacon and chop. Butter the base of a baking dish. Peel and chop onion finely. Core and chop the apple. In the baking dish, alternate slices of celeriac with a mixture of bacon, apple and onion. Add the white wine, mixed with cream, seasoning and nutmeg. Pour over the dish. Push in the walnut kernels. Bake in a very hot oven for 15 to 20 minutes.

COURGETTES

Courgette and tarragon soup

(E. Glass – The Roydon Cookery Book)

Ingredients

1lb/500g courgettes – trimmed but not peeled	**½ teaspoon tarragon leaves**
1 medium potato, chopped	**1pt/½ litre chicken stock**
1 small spring onion, chopped	**A little butter and oil**
	Salt and pepper

Fry the onion gently in the oil and butter until soft but still translucent. Add the other ingredients, stir and simmer gently till soft. Liquidise. Season. This soup is quite green and rather thick so add milk to your liking. Serve with croutons or cream.

Courgettes with minted butter

Boil courgettes and toss them in a butter made with a little chopped mint, a squeeze of lemon and a hint of fresh garlic, salt and pepper.

LEEK

Leek soup

Ingredients for 4

1lb/500g leeks	**A knob of butter**
2 good size potatoes	**2 bayleaves**
2pt/1 litre chicken stock	**Salt and pepper**

Clean the leeks and cut in slices. Peel and slice the potatoes. Melt the butter in a heavy saucepan, stir in the leeks without browning. When translucent, add potatoes, chicken stock and bayleaves. Cool until tender. Remove bayleaves, liquidise. Serve with a touch of cream and a sprinkling of chopped chervil.

Stuffed leek and potato pie

Ingredients for 4

4 large leeks	**A cupful of fresh breadcrumbs**
¾lb/300g lean ground pork	**½ teaspoon thyme**
1 onion, chopped	**¼pt/⅛ litre chicken stock**
2 tomatoes	**Butter**
1lb/500g potatoes	**Salt and pepper**

Preheat the oven to 400F, 200C, gas mark 6

Clean and blanch the leeks. Drain well. Mix the chopped onion with pork, thyme and seasoning. Open leeks lengthwise ¾ of the way and carefully spoon in the stuffing. Butter the base of an oven proof dish. Lay the leeks in it, pour chicken stock over them, cover with foil and bake for 30 minutes.

In the meantime, peel, boil and mash the potatoes leaving them quite firm. Bring the oven heat up to 450F, 230C, gas mark 8. Remove foil from the dish. Spoon out excess stock. Spread with a layer of mashed potatoes. Slice tomatoes, removing the seeds. Lay over potatoes, sprinkle with breadcrumbs. Dot with a few pieces of butter. Place in oven for 10 minutes until golden brown.

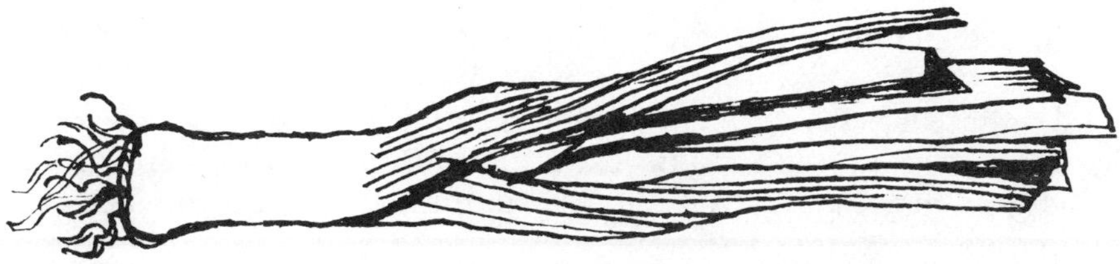

MARROW

Marrow duet

Slices of marrow, delicately stuffed, some with spinach and ham, others with basil tomatoes. Serve a slice of each with roast or grilled meat or poultry, or alternate the slices on a baking dish, sprinkle with grated cheese and serve as a main course.

Ingredients for tomato stuffing

4 to 6 tomatoes, peeled and chopped
1 onion, finely chopped
A few basil leaves
Salt and pepper
A little butter and oil for frying

Fry onion in butter and oil until translucent. Add the chopped tomatoes, seasoning and basil. Cook briefly and keep warm.

Ingredients for spinach and ham stuffing

8oz/250g fresh spinach
1 thick slice East Anglian ham
1 cup white sauce
Salt and pepper
Nutmeg

Blanch the spinach for 10 minutes. Drain well, chop with knife and fork, mix with white sauce and ham. Add seasoning and nutmeg. Keep warm.

Trim both ends of marrow and carefully scoop out seeds. Boil in salted water until tender. When cooked and well drained, cut in regular circular slices. Spoon a different stuffing in the middle of each slice.

MUSHROOMS

Low in calories and high in protein and minerals, this vegetable is sadly, like watercress, too often treated as a garnish. And yet it is grown fresh all year round and can be bought in four forms (button, cup, open cup of flat).

This means of course, that a diversity of dishes can be prepared with mushrooms as the main ingredient. Do not overcook mushrooms – they then lose colour, texture and food value.

Mushroom soup

8oz/250g button mushrooms
2pt/1 litre chicken stock
2oz/60g butter
1 dessertspoon flour
½ teaspoon lemon juice
2 dessertspoon thick cream
1 tablespoon chopped chervil
Salt and pepper

Using a heavy saucepan, melt the butter. When it froths add the sliced mushrooms. Stir well for 5 minutes. Sprinkle flour over vegetables, stirring constantly. Add chicken stock, a little at a time to avoid lumps. Now add the seasoning. Cook for a further 5 minutes. Liquidise, add cream, chervil and lemon juice. Reheat slowly.

Mushrooms on horseback

To serve with drinks or a chilled bottle of East Anglian wine.

Ingredients

Close cup mushrooms
Thin rashers of streaky bacon
Garlic butter
Cayenne pepper

Never wash or peel cultivated mushrooms. Just wipe clean with a damp cloth. Stir fry the mushrooms in garlic butter. Grill the bacon. Wrap bacon around each mushroom. Secure with a wooden skewer. Sprinkle with cayenne pepper and serve at once.

Ramequin of mushroom with sour cream

A good first course. Serve with Melba toast

Ingredients

1lb/500g close cup mushrooms
2oz/60g butter
A dash of Worcestershire sauce
A pinch of mace
1 teaspoon chopped chives
1 pot sour cream

Quarter the mushrooms, stir fry quickly in butter. Add seasoning and herbs and stir in sour cream and Worcestershire sauce. Pile in individual ramequin dishes. Serve at once, seasoned with salt and pepper.

A breakfast of mushrooms

Ingredients for 4

8oz/250g button mushrooms
2oz/60g butter
4 eggs
Pepper and salt

Preheat the oven to 400°F, 200°C, gas mark 6

Quickly fry the mushrooms in some of the butter without letting them take colour. Transfer in individual buttered ramequins. Break egg over each portion. Season with salt and pepper. Dot with a knob of butter and bake in oven in a roasting pan half filled with water until egg white is set.

A pan of mushrooms

Delicious with lots of granary bread. Can be eaten at any time from brunch to supper.

Ingredients for 4

1lb/500g open cup of flat mushrooms
2oz/60g butter
Chopped parsley, chives and chervil
½ clove of garlic
1 glass East Anglian white wine
Salt and pepper

Cut mushrooms in large pieces. Melt butter in a frying pan. As soon as it bubbles, add mushrooms and stir for 5 minutes. Add herbs, white wine and seasoning. Cover. Simmer for another 5 minutes. The mushrooms will give out their juice which will mix with the flavour of wine and herbs.

ONION

Spring onion soup

A good way of using the white and green of spring onions when they become too large for salad

Ingredients for 4

12 spring onions
6 outer leaves of lettuce
1 large potato
1oz/30g butter
1pt/½ litre chicken stock
2 dessertspoons single cream
1 dessertspoon chopped chives
Salt and pepper

Melt butter in a saucepan, add the roughly chopped lettuce leaves and the spring onions. Stir for a few minutes. Now add the peeled and sliced potato, chicken stock, salt and pepper. Simmer for 15 minutes. Liquidise. Reheat adding the cream and chopped chives.

Onion and gooseberry relish

Serve with cold meat or cheese

1lb/500g onions
½lb/250g large gooseberries
1 tablespoon fresh redcurrants
2 tablespoon oil
1 capful wine vinegar
A little sweet cicely
A few coriander seeds
¼ teaspoon freshly ground ginger
½ teaspoon grated lemon rind
Cayenne pepper
Plenty of coarsely ground pepper
Salt

Peel and slice the onions finely. Saute them in oil until translucent. Add the trimmed gooseberries and redcurrants, sweet cicely, coriander, lemon rind, ginger and seasoning. Add vinegar. Reduce heat and cook uncovered until mixture takes a jam consistency. Leave to cool.

PARSNIP

Thick parsnip winter soup

Ingredients

8 parsnips	**1 middle veal marrow bone**
4 carrots	**Salt and pepper**
1 onion	**2pt/1 litre water.**
A bunch of herbs, tied	

Clean, trim and peel the vegetables. Place in a heavy saucepan with stock, herbs and seasoning. Add the marrow bone. Bring to the boil and simmer gently for 2 hours. Remove herbs and bone but leave the marrow in the stock. Liquidise with a fresh sprinkling of white pepper. Serve very hot with crusty bread spread with butter and a touch of strong plain mustard.

PEA

Summer pea soup

Ingredients for 4

1lb/500g shelled peas	**2oz/60g butter**
1 lettuce heart	**2 large spring onions**
1 handful spinach	**Salt and pepper**
A sprig of mint	**2pt/1 litre chicken stock**

Melt butter in a heavy saucepan and when it bubbles add lettuce and spring onions. Cover and simmer for 5 minutes. Now add peas, spinach and mint as well as seasoning and stock. Bring to the boil, reduce heat, and simmer for 15 minutes. Liquidise. Serve with a swirl of yogurt and decorate with a mint leaf.

Peas and new potatoes with tarragon butter

Ingredients for 4

1lb/500g new potatoes, peeled	**2 sprigs of tarragon**
½lb/250g shelled peas	**2oz/60g butter**

Boil peas and potatoes separately. When tender, toss together with butter, seasoning and chopped tarragon leaves. Serve with grilled or roast meat.

POTATO

Herb soup

Ingredients for 4

4 large potatoes
1 onion, sliced
1pt/½ litre milk
1pt/½ litre chicken stock
3 tablespoons of chopped parsley, chervil, chives and lovage
A handful of crispy, chopped grilled bacon
A large knob of butter
Salt and pepper

Peel and slice the potatoes. Place in pan with onion, chicken stock, salt and pepper. Simmer until potatoes are tender. Liquidise with milk and herbs. Bring back to the pan, simmer for a further 5 minutes. Add butter, serve decorated with chopped bacon.

Potato, broad bean and bacon patties

Ingredients for 4

1 large potato, cooked
A handful of broadbeans, cooked
2 rashers sweet-cured bacon
1 egg, beaten
1 large spring onion, grated
Pepper

Fry the bacon slices until quite crisp. Reserve fat. Remove skin from broad beans and mash together with potato. Crumble the bacon and blend in the vegetable mixture with egg, onion and pepper. Form into balls, flatten into patties and fry in bacon fat until crisp on both sides. Serve with fried or poached eggs.

SPINACH

Spinach soup

Ingredients

1lb/500g fresh spinach
2 sorrel leaves (optional)
2oz/60g butter
1 small onion, finely sliced
1 tablespoon flour
1½pt/¾ litre chicken stock
Finely chopped hard boiled egg
Sour cream or yogurt

Wash spinach and sorrel leaves. In a heavy saucepan, melt the butter with the onion slices. Stir in the flour. Slowly add the chicken stock, stirring well to avoid lumps. Now add spinach and sorrel. Bring to the boil, reduce heat and simmer over gentle heat for roughly 15 minutes. Liquidise. Serve decorated with a swirl of sour cream or yogurt and chopped hard boiled egg.

Spinach omelette

A splendid quick meal with a tomato and onion salad, crusty bread and a glass of chilled East Anglian white wine.

Ingredients for 4

6 eggs
8oz/250g cooked leaf spinach
2 rashers smoked streaky bacon
2 thick slices brown bread
Butter
Salt and pepper
A few onion slices, thin
1 tablespoon of lukewarm water.

Fry the bacon rashers in a little butter. Divide in thin strips. Cube the bread and fry in same fat. Warm spinach through in a little butter while you make the omelette. Beat eggs with seasoning. Add a spoonful of lukewarm water for a very light omelette. Melt butter in frying pan, as soon as it bubbles pour in the eggs. Cook until set lifting the egg mixture with a spatula for lightness.
For the filling: Mix together spinach, bacon pieces and croutons. Check

seasoning. Spoon in the centre of omelette. Fold the omelette around the mixture and transfer to a serving dish.

TOMATO

Midsummer soup

Serve hot or cold. In both cases, the clear consistency combined with the sharp tang of the fruit creates a very refreshing taste.

Ingredients for 4

2lbs/1kg large tomatoes	**1 tablespoon olive oil**
1 large spring onion, sliced	**6 tarragon leaves, chopped**
¼ cucumber	**1pt/½ litre chicken stock**

Peel the tomatoes after dipping them in warm water for a few minutes. Chop them roughly and place in saucepan with oil, stock, onion and seasoning. Add the tarragon leaves. Cook for 8 to 10 minutes. Liquidise. Adjust seasoning. Serve with very thin slices of cucumber, hot or chilled.

Stuffed tomatoes

This recipe has been written at the request of Peter Harrison, manager of Grimsby Exchange Ltd.

Ingredients for 4

8 large tomatoes	**1 egg**
1lb/500g ground pork	**Salt and pepper**
1 tablespoon fresh parsley, chopped	**1 glass of East Anglian dry white wine**
1 onion, chopped finely	

One hour before preparing the dish, cut top off tomatoes. Scoop out seeds. Turn the hollowed tomatoes upside down to drain off any excess fluid. In the meantime, prepare the stuffing – the flavour will improve if the ingredients are chilled together for a while. Using a fork mix the ground pork with beaten egg, seasoning, chopped onion and parsley. Refrigerate for 1 hour.

Preheat the oven to 425F, 220C, gas mark 7

Season the inside of each tomato with a touch of salt and pepper. Press the meat stuffing into each one. Cover with tomato tops. Dot a small knob of butter on each tomato and bake for 45 minutes. Pour the wine in the baking dish. Cook for a further 10 minutes, basting once or twice.

P.S. Tomatoes cooked this way are very good cold. In which case, omit the wine towards the end of cooking to keep them as dry as possible. Chill overnight and serve at a picnic.

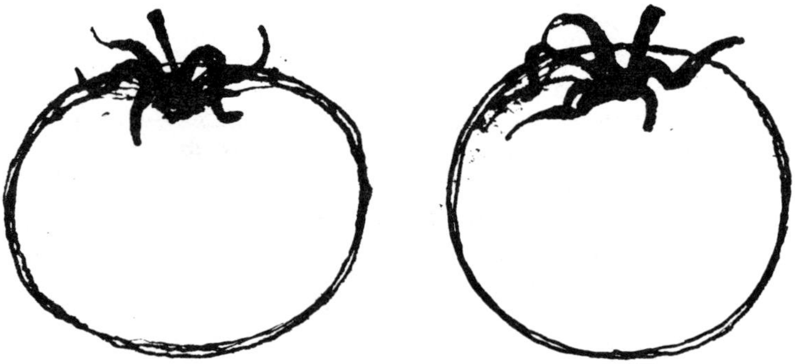

TURNIP

The all East Anglian mash

A very visual dish of mashed potatoes, peas, turnips and carrots. Puree each vegetable with butter and seasoning, leaving quite firm. Then serve as four colourful stripes in a long dish, with roast or grilled meat.

Salads

A bowl of salad is a bowl of health. Especially in East Anglia where such varied products are on everyone's doorstep. There are so many combinations and young vegetables are often a good and healthy addition. There are small asparagus tips, which you need not cook, young carrots, rich in vitamin C and A, cabbage, spinach, young peas and, of course, raw mushrooms. Some fresh fruit marries well with salads, and dressings can vary with each salad. Here are a few suggestions for salad dressings.

Oil and vinegar dressing: 3 measures of oil to 1 small measure of vinegar, salt and pepper.

Mustard dressing: of itself varies in taste according to the mustard used. Make it with 3 measures of oil, ½ measure vinegar, ½ teaspoon mustard, salt and pepper

Citrus dressing: As a substitute for vinegar use a good teaspoon of lemon juice

Cream dressing: 3 tablespoons of sour cream, chopped chives, lemon juice, salt and pepper

Copella's dressing: 100ml Copella apple juice, 25ml sunflower oil, juice of ½ lemon, ½ teaspoon grain mustard, Tamari or soya sauce, pepper and oregano to taste

Queen Adelaide tomato salad dressing: Oil, lemon, salt and pepper, a pinch of fresh thyme, a pinch of sweet basil, a few ground dry lovage seeds

Salads suggestions

Louth salad

In honour of the British Quality Vegetable and Salad Association, here is a salad which combines salad products as well as many of the traditional vegetables grown in East Anglia

1 lettuce
2 tomatoes
2 celery sticks
1 small raw beetroot, peeled and grated
2 carrots, peeled and grated
½ green pepper, thinly sliced
2 small courgettes, trimmed and sliced
1 young turnip, grated
6 button mushrooms, sliced
A few green beans, blanched
1 tablespoon of young raw peas, shelled
A few sprigs of young cauliflower
A few radishes for decoration
½ bunch watercress
2 shallots, chopped

Decorate the base of salad bowl with large lettuce leaves. Combine other ingredients. Accomodate with herbs and dressing of your choice. Pile on to the lettuce leaves and decorate with the radishes.

Norfolk salad

Mange-tout peas
Button mushrooms
Spring onions
A few young asparagus tips

Blanch mange-tout peas for 5 minutes in salted water. Rinse under cold tap. Leave to cool. When cool, mix with sliced raw mushrooms and asparagus. Season with a light mustard dressing.

Cottage green salad

8oz/250g plain cottage cheese
½ lettuce
¼ cucumber
A few spinach leaves, raw
1 bunch watercress
Chives
2 mint leaves
Chervil and parsley
2 tablespoons single cream or sour cream
1 teaspoon vinegar
Salt and pepper

Dice the cucumber without peeling it. Chop roughly lettuce, spinach and watercress. Chop herbs finely. Mix salt, pepper and vinegar with the single cream. Fold in with cheese, salad vegetables and herbs. Eat chilled, on its own with crusty bread.

Orchard salad

2 carrots
A few radishes
1 large spring onion
¼ white cabbage
¼lb/120g stoned cherries
1 pear
1 apple

Slice the spring onion, shred the cabbage, dice the carrots and slice the radishes. Combine with the cherries, pear and apple chopped but not peeled. Serve with Copella's dressing.

Queen Adelaide tomato salad

6 large ripe tomatoes	**2 large spring onions**
2 hard boiled eggs	

Slice the tomatoes, remove the seeds. Alternate on a shallow dish with slices of hard boiled egg and onions. Serve with Queen Adelaide dressing (see page 147).

Market gardener potato salad

1lb/500g small new potatoes	**2 large spring onions, chopped**
6 sticks celery, chopped	**1 green pepper, chopped**
6 hard boiled eggs, chopped	**lovage, dill**

Cook potatoes and cut in thin slices. When cool, combine with other salad vegetables. Season with a cream and mustard dressing, chopped lovage leaves and a small amount of dill.

Curried winter salad

1 lettuce	**2 tablespoons grated celeriac, raw**
3 chicory	**1 tablespoon chopped walnuts**
1 cooked beetroot, peeled and sliced	**1 eating apple**
	Lemon juice

Core and slice the apple but do not peel. Trim and divide the chicory in strips. Toss in lemon juice with the grated celeriac to avoid bruising.

Garnish the bottom of a salad bowl with lettuce leaves. Chop the lettuce heart. Combine all the ingredients with a dressing made of plain yogurt, salt and pepper, a little coriander and ¼ teaspoon of mild curry powder.

Calluna Farm salad

This salad was made on my return from visiting Helen Douglas who, at her farm in Hollesley near Woodbridge, makes an excellent cheese from sheep's milk: the Peppered Colony.

1 frisee endive	**2 crushed basil leaves**
4 tomatoes	**Slices of Peppered Colony cheese**

Wash the endive, pat dry and arrange on a flat dish. Slice the tomatoes and place on top. Layer the cheese slices in the middle. Sprinkle with crushed basil. Pour on a citrus dressing made with olive oil. Simply enjoy this salad on its own with crusty bread and East Anglian wine.

Finally . . . a dip to be served with crisp strips of carrots, celery, cucumber etc. . .

Norwich Market dip

1lb/500g large peas, cooked	**½lb/250g cream cheese**
2 teaspoons fresh mint sauce	**1 tablespoon sour cream**
1 onion, grated	**Salt and pepper**

Mash the peas while hot. Leave to cool and chill, seasoned with mint sauce. Add onion, cream cheese and sour cream. Adjust seasoning. Serve as suggested.

Desserts, Cakes & Bread

Desserts, Cakes & Bread

If East Anglia has never gained a gastronomic reputation for its cheeses, the region is very much on the map when it comes to the making of desserts, cakes, bread, jams and preserves. Between the vast yearly production of wheat for flour, beet for sugar, eggs from quality poultry farming and acres of fruit farms scattered all over the region, how could it be otherwise?

Wisbech and Essex are great centres for soft fruit such as strawberries, raspberries, gooseberries, black and redcurrants. Indigenous species of plums, apples and pears are still to be found in each county and every year, students, housewives and entire families will spend a budget holiday in East Anglia helping to harvest fruit.

It is not surprising, therefore, to find old established family names such as Elsenham or Wilkin and Sons of Tiptree on the list of East Anglian jam and preserves manufacturers. There are also more recent success stories such as Cartwright and Butler, Culpeper or Mr Bumbles preserves made to order and sold in America.

In recent years, many 'pick your own' fruit farms and orchards have opened their door to the public and, for city dwellers who do not have the benefit of a fruit tree in their own garden, Olivers Orchard, near Colchester have gone a step further. Their 'pick a tree' scheme enables families to own and harvest the tree of their choice in this luscious farm, cleverly run by Rupert and Jennifer Knowles.

There is good quality honey to be found. Pure apple and grape juices are prepared in Suffolk and Essex, and in Lincolnshire, elderflowers and raspberries are processed into delectable cordials at Belvoir Fruit Farms.

Old family traditional recipes are there to be reproduced or tampered with and, with a little imagination and a cool glass of dessert wine, these excellent raw or processed products can become the happy finale of any East Anglian meal.

APPLES

A breakfast of apples

This is excellent prepared the previous day, kept cool overnight and served, cold with single cream and cups of lemon tea. An easy breakfast when entertaining guests.

Ingredients for 4

4 thick slices of fruit loaf	**2lbs/1kg dessert apples**
2 tablespoons soft brown sugar	**A pinch of cinnamon**
2oz/60g unsalted butter	**½ teaspoon grated lemon rind**
A few sultanas	**1 glass pure apple juice**

Peel, core and slice the apples in regular size slices. Place in a heavy, flameproof pan with sugar, peel, cinnamon and sultanas. Pour apple juice over, cover and cook gently until tender. Fry the bread slices in butter until golden on both sides. While still warm spoon apples over the bread with slotted spoon. Leave to cool.

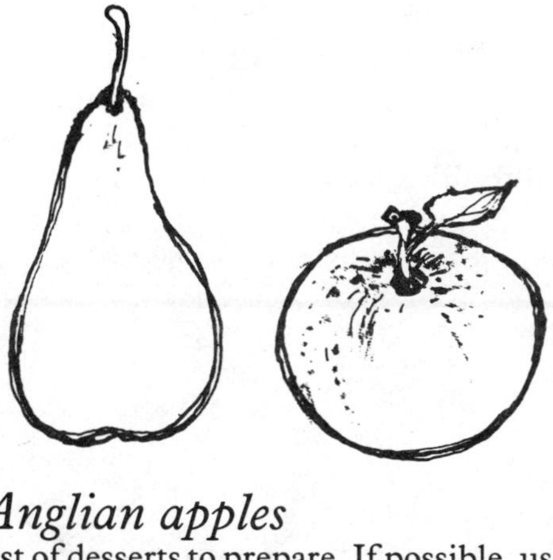

Tipsy East Anglian apples

Probably the easiest of desserts to prepare. If possible, use D'Arcy Spice apples. Grown in East Anglia since 1880 when they were first found at the Hall in the village of Tolleshunt D'Arcy, in Essex, these late russets are best not picked before November and will keep until May. Their crisp texture, their pleasantly aromatic taste, blend well with the flowery East Anglian wine.

Preheat the oven to 450F, 230C, gas mark 8

Butter an ovenproof dish, slice and core but do not peel the apples. Lay the apple slices overlapping in the dish. Sprinkle with soft brown sugar, dot with small pieces of unsalted butter and pour a good glass of medium dry or sweet East Anglian wine over the fruit. Bake until tender. Serve from the dish with single cream.

East Anglian bread pudding

Ingredients for 4

4 large apples of the same size
6oz/180g stale bread or fruit loaf
4 glasses of milk
4oz/120g soft brown sugar
1 lemon
3 eggs
Grated lemon rind
1 large glass of pure apple juice
A little unsalted butter

Preheat the oven to 425F, 220C, gas mark 7

Peel and core the apples but leave them whole. Place them in a heavy pan together with 2oz/60g brown sugar, apple juice and a little lemon juice. Cook gently, uncovered for 10 to 15 minutes until soft. In the meantime, bring the milk to the boil and pour over the bread in a mixing bowl. When the bread is soft, mash it in the milk with a fork. Add the remaining sugar, the lemon rind and the beaten eggs.

Butter an oblong baking dish. Pour the bread mixture into it, and push in the baked apples. Spoon the cooking juices over the fruit, dot with butter and bake for 30 minutes. Serve from the dish with single cream.

Open apple and quince tart

It may sound a little fiddly to prepare but the result is well worth the effort.

Ingredients

For the pastry	For the filling
8oz/250g flour	**2 large quinces**
5oz/150g unsalted butter	**2 large dessert apples**
A pinch of salt	**2oz/60g flaked almonds**
A small glass of lukewarm water.	**10oz/300g sugar**
	Vanilla pod

Make the pastry, leave it in a cold room for 1 to 2 hours.

Start on the garnish: Peel the quinces and cut out the centre. Divide the fruit longways in quarters. Cook the quince peel and the core in a little water for 15 to 20 minutes. Sieve, place the flavoured liquid into a saucepan with sugar and vanilla pod. Poach the quince in this syrup for 25 minutes or until tender. Drain with slotted spoon and cool. Reduce syrup to half by boiling it, leave to cool.

Preheat the oven to 425F, 220C, gas mark 7

Now roll pastry and line a tart dish with it. Sprinkle the flaked almonds over the pastry. Slice and core the apples. Slice the poached quinces. Alternate the two fruit inside the dish in a circular pattern. Sprinkle with a little sugar and cook for 30 minutes. When cooked, glaze the tart with the quince syrup. Leave to cool slightly and serve with cream, lightly whipped with castor sugar and grated lemon rind.

Apple batter pudding with wine sauce

A nourishing winter dessert.

Ingredients

1lb/500g dessert apples	**4 eggs**
2oz/60g flour	**4oz/120g sugar**
1 mug of milk	**Butter**
1 teaspoon finely grated lemon rind	**A pinch of salt**

Preheat the oven to 400F, 200C, gas mark 6

In a mixing bowl, sift flour and sugar with the salt. Add the beaten eggs then the milk, slowly stirring well. Add lemon rind. Peel, core and slice the apples thinly. Mix them with the batter. Butter generously an ovenproof dish. Pour the mixture in it and bake for 40 minutes. When cooked and golden brown, serve, sliced with wine sauce.

For the sauce:

4oz/100g unsalted butter
2 tablespoons East Anglian sweet white wine
Lemon rind, grated
Sugar

Mix the ingredients together. Boil until it reduces and serve over the batter pudding.

Caramel apple cream

A refreshing tangy family secret, served with single or light sour cream

Ingredients

1½lb/750g sharp cooking apples
3oz/90g unsalted butter
4oz/120g castor sugar
1 lemon
3 eggs
1 dessertspoon flour

Preheat the oven to 325F, 170C, gas mark 3.
Grate the lemon rind very finely. Peel, slice and core the apples. Place in a saucepan with sugar and lemon rind. Cover and simmer very gently until tender. Puree the apples with unsalted butter, add flour and mix well. Now add the beaten eggs, one by one. Make the caramel by melting 2oz/60g castor sugar with 1 dessertspoon of water in a deep round cake tin. As soon as the caramel starts taking colour, hold the tin in both hands with oven gloves and, turning slowly clockwise, coat the sides of tin with the caramel. Leave to cool.

Pour the apple mixture inside the caramelised mould. Place in a bain-marie and bake in oven for 40 minutes. The dessert is cooked when a knife blade comes out clean when inserted in the middle. Chill overnight in the refrigerator. Turn on to a shallow serving dish. Serve with chilled dessert East Anglian wine.

PEARS

Fresh pears with crushed raspberries

A very refreshing summer dessert to be served on its own or with plain yogurt

Ingredients for 4

4 ripe pears
1 punnet raspberries
1 dessertspoon castor sugar
1 lemon
Fresh mint to decorate

Chill pears and raspberries until just before preparation. Peel the pears and immediately squeeze ½ lemon juice over then to avoid bruising. Place the raspberries, castor sugar and remaining lemon juice in a food blender. Reduce to pulp. Serve spooned over pears and decorate with mint.

Almond pears with chocolate sauce

A rich winter dessert made with late season pears

Ingredients for 4

4 large pears
4oz/120g ground almonds
2oz/60g unsalted butter
3 dessertspoon honey
1oz/30g chopped candied orange peel
Juice of a lemon

For the chocolate sauce
5oz/150g dark chocolate
1 dessertspoon doublecream
1 small knob butter

Preheat the oven to 375F, 190C, gas mark 5
Peel the pears, divide them in halves and core with a spoon. Mix the ground almonds with honey, butter and orange peel. Fill the cavity with this mixture. Cover pears with foil and bake in oven until tender. Serve lukewarm with chocolate sauce, made by slowly melting the chocolate with the cream and butter.

Open pear tart

Ingredients for 4

8oz/250g flour
4oz/120g unsalted butter
1 dessertspoon ground almonds
2oz/60g castor sugar
1 pinch of salt
Water

For the filling
4 large pears
6oz/180g caster sugar
4 egg yolks
3½oz/100g butter, unsalted
1½oz/45g flour
½pt/¼ litre milk
½pt/¼ litre water
2 dessertspoons raspberry jelly

Make the pastry and chill for 1 hour. Preheat the oven to 425F, 220C, gas mark 7
Roll pastry in flan dish and bake blind for 20 to 25 minutes. In the meantime prepare the filling. Peel the pears, halve them and core. Poach until tender in a syrup made with water, 3oz/90g sugar and the vanilla pod. When cooked lift with slotted spoon and drain well.

Make the cream base: Bring the milk to boiling point with the vanilla pod. Leave to cool. Mix the egg yolks with sugar and flour. Remove vanilla pod from the milk, add the milk slowly to egg mixture, mixing well. Transfer the mixture to a saucepan and, stirring constantly, thicken over very low heat. Whisk in the butter, off the heat. Leave the cream to cool slightly, then spoon on to pastry base. Arrange half pears in a pattern over cream. Reduce the cooking pear syrup by half over high heat, mix with raspberry jelly. Pour over fruit. Serve cold.

Pear and chocolate truffles with white chocolate sauce

Cubes of spiced poached pears wrapped in a smooth truffle mixture. A very special dessert. Serve it either with the white chocolate sauce or, for a sharp contrast with unsweetened sour cream.

Peel, core and quarter full flavoured pears. Poach them in a syrup made of ½pt/¼ litre water, 3oz/90g sugar, a touch of ginger, a touch of cinnamon, a vanilla pod. Do not overcook – the pears should stay firm. Drain well with slotted spoon, cut in large cubes and reserve cooking syrup for the sauce.

Ingredients for 12 truffles

4oz/120g best quality dark chocolate	**1 egg yolk**
1 dessertspoon milk	**1½oz/45g unsalted butter**
	2 dessertspoon thick cream

Slowly melt the chocolate with the milk. Off the heat, whisk in the butter little by little, then add the egg yolk and the cream. Leave to cool and chill for 1 hour. Shape chocolate mixture into 12 balls. With thumb, make an indentation into the chocolate. Fill with pieces of pears, close opening. Chill.

For the sauce you will need:

5oz/150g white chocolate	**1 teaspoon freshly grated orange or tangerine rind**
2 tablespoons double cream	
1 tablespoon pear syrup	

Melt the chocolate slowly with the cream and syrup. Add the rind. Chill. To serve, spoon the chocolate sauce on individual plates. Place 3 chilled pear truffles in the middle. Dust with cocoa powder.

PLUMS

Spicy plum fool

Ingredients

2lbs/1kg plums	**½ teaspoon cinnamon**
2 dessertspoons castor sugar	**¼ teaspoon ground nutmeg**
8oz/250g whipping cream	**A small glass of water**
1 dessertspoon brandy	

Bring water and sugar to the boil and add the plums. Cover and simmer for 10 minutes. Remove the plums with a slotted spoon. Discard stones. Chill. Before serving, whip cream. Add brandy, cinnamon and nutmeg. Fold in the plums. Serve, chilled in individual glasses with macaroons.

'Norfolk Punch' plums

The original 'Olde Norfolk Punch', a mysteriously herby medieval drink is still today concocted at Welle Manor Hall, Upwell, in the Norfolk fens. Quite apart from proudly claiming 21 health-giving properties, it is a very pleasant non-alcoholic drink, not dissimilar to the taste of mulled wine. It gives a delicious flavour to stewed Victoria plums. I like to serve this dessert chilled with yogurt or sour cream.

Ingredients

1lb/500g Victoria plums
2 glass Norfolk Punch
1 vanilla pod
1 teaspoon liquid honey
A little arrowroot

Place plums, Norfolk Punch, vanilla pod and honey in a saucepan. Cover and simmer gently until plums are tender. Remove the vanilla pod. Remove plums with a slotted spoon. Discard the stones. Add a little arrowroot to the cooking juices and thicken. Chill fruit and juice, separately, overnight. Serve in individual glasses. Spoon sauce over the fruit.

Cambridge greengage with lemon cream

The honey-taste green plum was first introduced in this country by Sir William Gage – hence the name. It is still found in the region and often known as Cambridge gage. The taste of the fruit when ripe is so subtle it does not deserve to be too much tampered with. Just stew the fruit with a little honey over very low heat until tender. Leave to cool. Discard stones. Press with a fork into individual ramequins. Chill overnight. Serve, turned on to individual plates, topped with cream lightly whipped with the finely grated rind of a lemon.

SOFT FRUIT

Midsummer Medley

Ingredients

1lb/500g strawberries
½lb/250g raspberries
½lb/250g cherries
4oz/120g blackcurrants
4oz/120g redcurrants
6 tablespoons redcurrant jelly
1 lemon
Water

Stone the cherries. Trim other fruit, hull the strawberries. Place in a fruit bowl. In a saucepan melt slowly the redcurrant jelly with a cup of water and a squeeze of lemon juice. Pour over the fruit. Chill for a few hours. Serve with cream or yogurt.

Fresh raspberry crush

Crush together 1lb/500g raspberries with 3½oz/100g of caster sugar and a little lemon juice. Chill. Spoon at the last minute over plain vanilla ice cream or blancmange.

Rhubarb and raspberry tart

This recipe was kindly given by Mrs M. Osborn, Beechamwell, Norfolk.

Line a pie dish with pastry made with lard or margarine. Strip the outer skin of rhubarb, hull the raspberries. Put a layer of rhubarb over the pastry, sprinkle with a little sugar. Now add the raspberries, more rhubarb and a little more sugar. Cover with pastry. Make a slit in the centre and bake in warm oven for ¾ hour to one hour.

East Anglian wine mousse

Ingredients

1pt/½ litre East Anglian medium dry wine
8oz/250g castor sugar
4 eggs
3 small lemons
½oz/15g cornflour
1 punnet raspberries

Separate white from yolks of eggs. Cream together the 4 egg yolks with the cornflour and a little wine. Add slowly the juice and grated rind of lemons, then the wine. Whisk well. Thicken the mixture over very low heat, whisking all the time. As soon as it takes a good creamy consistency, take off the heat. Whisk egg white until very firm and fold gently into the wine custard. Spoon into individual glasses, chill and serve topped with fresh raspberries. This dessert cannot be prepared too long in advance or it would separate.

Southend fruit coquilles

Originally they were made in the shells of cockles or scallops. Tin or pyrex versions are now on the market. Make a sponge mixture. Divide it into well greased scallop dishes. When cooked, leave to cool. Slice in half but not right through. Fill with cold raspberries and blackcurrants which have been cooked with a little sugar and lemon juice. Serve with whipped cream. Decorate with fruit leaves.

Bacchus cream with frosted blackcurrants

Ingredients

1pt/½ litre East Anglian dessert wine
3½oz/100g castor sugar
A pinch of cinnamon
5 egg yolks
Caramel (see page 156)

For the blackcurrant topping
2 egg whites
4oz/120g fresh blackcurrants on their stalks
6oz/180g crystallised sugar

Preheat oven to 350F, 180C, gas mark 4
In a saucepan, bring to the boil white wine with sugar and cinnamon. Leave to cool. When cool, pour slowly, stirring well, over the 5 beaten egg yolks. Strain through a nylon sieve and pour into a caramelised tin or mould. Bake in a bain-marie in the oven for 15 minutes or until set. Leave to cool and chill.

Turn on to a serving plate topped with the frosted blackcurrants. To frost, beat the 2 egg whites, place sugar in a saucer. Dip the blackcurrants in the egg white, then in the crystallised sugar. Arrange on centre of cream, decorate with blackcurrant leaves.

Strawberry meringue tart

This tart is especially delicious made with alpine strawberries, but any small strong tasting species will do. Note that the pastry is quite different.

Ingredients

For the pastry
8oz/250g flour
4oz/120g good quality unsalted butter
1 tablespoon milk
1 tablespoon castor sugar
1 small measure Brandy

For the filling
8oz/250g strawberries
4oz almond flakes
Raspberry jelly
4 egg whites
6 tablespoons castor sugar
½ teaspoon lemon juice

Preheat the oven to 425F, 220C, gas mark 7
Make pastry. Leave to chill for one hour. Roll out and bake blind until just cooked but not too brown. Lower the heat to 325F, 170C, gas mark 3.

Grill almond flakes. Spread a little raspberry jelly over the base of the cooked pastry. Sprinkle almonds over it. Whisk egg whites until firm, add lemon juice and sugar and fold in strawberries, left whole. Spoon into the pastry case and bake for roughly 30 minutes or until the meringue has taken good colour.

East Anglian strawberry cup

Ingredients

1lb/500g strawberries
2 dessertspoons of sugar
1 bottle East Anglian rose wine
The grated rind of an orange
12 mint leaves

Prepare the mint leaves ice cubes: half fill ice cube tray with water, lay mint leaves on top, place in freezer to set. When set, fill to top and re-freeze. Hull the strawberries, place them in a fruit bowl. Sprinkle with sugar and grated orange rind. Pour wine over the fruit. Chill for 1 hour. Serve in fruit or punch bowl with mint iced cubes scattered among the fruit.

Gooseberry solid syllabub

Ingredients

8oz/250g gooseberries
½pt/¼ litre East Anglian white wine
1 teaspoon finely grated lemon rind
A touch of sweet cicely
4 egg yolks
1oz/15g cornflour
4oz/120g sugar
4oz/120g whipped cream

Trim gooseberries and cook them slowly with sweet cicely. Leave to cool. Bring the wine to the boil with sugar and lemon rind. Leave to cool slightly. In a mixing bowl, cream the egg yolks with the cornflour, add the spiced wine slowly, stirring well. Transfer to a pan and, whisking all the time, cook over gentle heat until the cream thickens. Add the fruit puree to this preparation. When cooled, fold in the whipped cream. Serve chilled, in individual glasses.

Other desserts

Culpeper blossom dessert

Mix plain yogurt with 1 tablespoon whipped cream. Spoon into a glass and top with a layer of any of the exquisite Culpeper's blossom jellies (elderflower, rose petal or cowslip). Serve well chilled, with brandy snaps.

Norfolk treacle tart

One of the many pleasures of the Dickensian table, so marvellously evoked by *Cedric Dickens, Charles Dicken's great-grandson in his book 'Dining with Dickens'.*

Ingredients

4oz/120g rich shortcrust pastry to line tin
Butter, knob size of a walnut
Grated lemon rind
4 tablespoons golden syrup
2 tablespoons cream
1 small beaten egg

Warm syrup gently, add butter in small pieces off the heat to dissolve. Add the cream, grated rind and beaten egg. Put in the pastry lined tin and bake in a moderate oven for 25–30 minutes. Prick when setting begins.

CARROT DESSERTS

In a region where the carrot is king, I am delighted to include a few carrot desserts in this chapter. I personally adore the moist consistency this root vegetable gives to any sweet preparation. The first recipe was given to me by an American kissing-cousin, a Tilleray from Virginia, U.S.A. posted at the Lakenheath American base at the time. It is a very moist cake, which seems much too liquid in consistency at the time of baking. Don't worry – the final result is ambrosia.

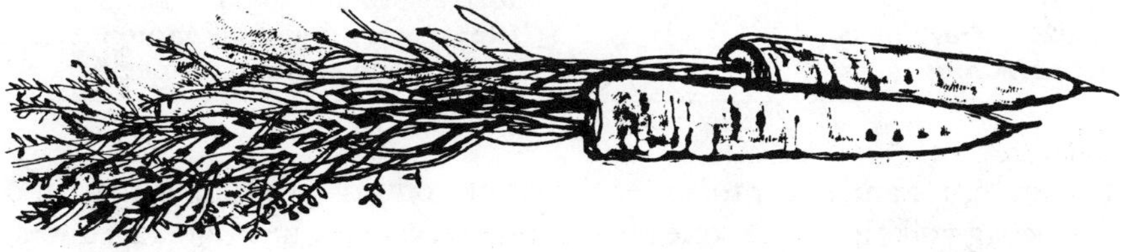

Tilleray carrot cake

Ingredients

2 cups grated raw carrots	**1 cup sunflower oil**
1½ cup self-raising flour	**3 eggs**
½ cup chopped almonds	**½ teaspoon cinnamon**
1 cup soft brown sugar	**Pinch of salt**

Preheat the oven to 325F, 170C, gas mark 3
Sift flour with salt and cinnamon. Using an electric whisk, blend together oil and sugar. Add eggs, one by one, then all of the flour at once. Beat for a while, then fold in carrots and nuts. Divide mixture between 2 greased sandwich tins. Bake for 1 hour or until well risen and spongy to the finger. Leave to cool in the tins for 10 minutes then turn on to wire rack.

Sandwich together with following filling:

4oz/120g cream cheese	**1 teaspoon vanilla essence**
4oz/120g good unsalted butter	**1 teaspoon finely grated lemon rind**
1 cup icing sugar	

Cream butter and cream cheese. Add icing sugar, beat well until frothy. Add vanilla and lemon rind.

Carrot pudding with syllabub sauce

Ingredients

8oz/250g carrots, finely grated	**8oz/250g unsalted butter**
4oz/120g chopped almonds of hazelnuts	**3 eggs**
8oz/250g fresh brown breadcrumbs	**4oz/120g castor sugar**
	1 teaspoon ground cinnamon
	¼ teaspoon ground nutmeg

Cream butter and sugar together. Separate yolks from white of eggs and whisk egg yolks in butter, one by one. Fold in carrots, nuts, breadcrumbs and spices. Whisk egg whites until firm and fold in lightly. Spoon into a well buttered pudding basin. Wrap with foil and steam for 2 hours.

Syllabub sauce

Ingredients

¼pt/⅛ litre sweet East Anglian white wine	**1 lemon**
2 eggs	**1oz/30g butter**
	2oz/60g East Anglian honey

While the pudding is cooking, soak together the wine with lemon juice and finely grated rind of lemon. Before serving, bring this liquid to the boil and let it boil for 7 minutes. Place the saucepan into a larger one half-filled with boiling water to create a bain-marie. Add honey and butter to the sauce, then add the well beaten eggs, stirring well until sauce thickens. The sauce is ready when it coats the back of a spoon. Serve at once with hot slices of carrot pudding.

Carrot fudge

Ingredients

1lb/500g carrots, grated fine	**A glass of milk**
1oz/30g sultanas	**2oz/60g unsalted butter**
1oz/30g raisins	**A few blanched almonds to decorate**
1oz/30g chopped walnuts	**A sprinkling of icing sugar**
1oz/30g chopped hazelnuts	
6oz/180g sugar	

Mix grated carrots with sugar and milk. Pour the mixture into a heavy non-stick frying pan and cook very slowly over low heat, stirring from time to time until all liquid has been absorbed. Add butter in small pieces, mixing well. Continue cooking over medium heat until mixture is tender. Blend in sultanas, raisins, nuts and cinnamon. Press the mixture into an oiled square dish and leave to cool. Divide in squares, press a blanched almond into each portion and sprinkle with a little icing sugar.

Suffolk mincemeat and Christmas pudding

Follow any rich mincemeat recipe but add ½ lb of grated carrots to the mixture. Do the same with Christmas pudding mixture. The final result is light and moist.

* * * * *

And to conclude this chapter, a cake, a bread and a rusk I made on my return from visiting three of the ancient mills, striking monuments scattered among the East Anglian countryside. One is the Downfield windmill at Soham, the other two are watermills, one at Letheringsett, near Holt, the other one, newly re-opened at Foulden.

To reach for a packet of flour on a shop shelf is a banal and everyday habit for a cookery writer but, when I drove back with the wholewheat flour from the traditional mills, I felt I had bags of gold in my shopping basket. This is no ordinary flour: the grain comes from the well-drained chalky fields around Newmarket where the terrain helps to produce very hard wheat, the only sort suitable for this kind of milling.

At the turn of a handle, the giant sails or waterwheels will set the grinding stones in motion, producing a minimum of 3 tons per week of natural 14% protein charged wholewheat flour. The bran can be kept in or sieved out of the flour, to the customer's choice.

Walnut wholewheat bread

Excellent with jam, butter, cheese and some of the recipes mentioned in this book.

Ingredients

2oz/60g fresh yeast	**3 tablespoon oil**
1¼pt/¾ litre water	**2lb/1kg wholewheat flour**
2 teaspoons salt	**6oz/180g walnut kernels**

Put sugar and yeast in a small bowl, add 2 tablespoons of lukewarm water, cover and set to froth in a warmish place. Mix remaining water, salt and oil together. Put the flour in a large mixing bowl. Make a well in the centre. Pour in the yeast and water/oil mixture. Blend with hands. When well mixed, the mixture should be coming away from the sides of the bowl.

Place the dough onto floured board and knead for 10 minutes until smooth. Shape dough in a ball and transfer in one piece to a greased plastic bag. Keep in warm place for one hour or until dough has almost doubled its size. Return dough to a floured board. Punch the air out of it and knead for 5 minutes. Insert the walnut kernels in the dough. Shape roughly with hands and half fill greased loaf tins with the mixture. Return to warm place for a further 30 minutes.

Preheat the oven to 475F, 240C, gas mark 9. Bake for 15 minutes, then lower the heat to 425F, 220C, gas mark 7 and bake for a further 20 minutes.

Suffolk rusk

Ingredients

8oz/250g wholewheat flour	**1 egg**
1 teaspoon baking powder	**A pinch castor sugar**
3oz/90g butter	**Water**

Preheat oven at 450F, 230C, gas mark 8
Sift flour with salt and baking powder. Rub fat in the mixture, add the sugar, beaten egg and just enough water to make a stiff dough. Roll out onto a floured board, divide in rounds 1 inch thick. Bake for 15 minutes. Lower the oven heat down to 350F, 180C, gas mark 4. Cut the rusks in half, return to the oven, open sides upwards. Bake until very crisp. Cool and serve with butter, cheese or other recipes mentioned earlier in the book. They will keep dry in a cake tin for a while.

Hedgerow sponge cake

Made with wholemeal flour, this cake is deliciously nutty. For the filling, I used a jam recipe compiled by Melanie Knibbs, a clever food scientist, whose delicious cakes and preserves can be found at markets and shops throughout north Norfolk.

Ingredients

½lb/250g wholemeal flour	**½lb/250g castor sugar**
1 teaspoonful baking powder	**4 eggs**
½lb/250g unsalted butter	**Pinch of salt**

Sift flour and salt together. Warm a mixing bowl and cream the butter and sugar until light and fluffy. Add the eggs, one at a time, beating well. Fold in half of the flour, mix well, then the other half. Divide the mixture into well greased and lightly floured cake tins. Bake in a preheated oven at 350F, 180C, gas mark 4 for about 20 minutes or until the blade of a knife comes out clean. Cool the cakes in the tin for a while, then turn onto a wire rack. When cold, spread one cake with hedgerow jam and place the other on top.

Hedgerow jam (from Melanie Knibbs)

Ingredients

1lb/500g elderberries	**4oz/125g hazelnuts**
1lb/500g blackberries	**3½lb/2kg sugar**
1lb/500g crabapples	**3 pints/1½ litres water**
8oz/250g sloes	

Peel, core and chop the crabapples and prick the sloes with a pin. Put all the fruit into a large pan with the water. Simmer until soft. Add the sugar and shelled hazelnuts, stirring until all the sugar has dissolved. Boil hard until set. The sloe stones should be removed if possible while the jam is cooking but some will probably remain in the jam.

Index by choice

Breakfast Dishes

Snacks With Drinks

Soups

First Course

Lunches and Snacks

Main Course

Vegetables

Salads

Desserts

Miscellaneous

Chapter Index

Shellfish

Fish

Game

Pork and Pork Products

Poultry

Beef and Lamb

Vegetables & Salads

Desserts, cakes & bread